CROSSING THE TERRIBLE WORLD-OCEAN

Michael Bajek

Crossing the Terrible World-Ocean
Copyright © Michael Bajek 2017

All rights reserved. No part of this publication may be reproduced, stored in a retrieval system, or transmitted in any form or by any means – electronic, mechanical, photocopying, recording, or otherwise – without the prior written permission of the author.

Introduction Commentaries by:
©Stephen N. Xenakis
©HarSimran Kaur
©Horatio Hernandez
All rights reserved

Front and back cover images from original oil paintings by © Barbara J. Bajek. All rights reserved.

First published in 2017 by Completely Novel in the United Kingdom.

ISBN: 9781787231344

The fearful ocean of the world is dangerous and formidable; it hath no shore or limit.

No boat, no raft, no pole, and no boatman;

But the true Guru hath a vessel for the terrible ocean, and ferrieth over him on whom he looketh with favor.

--Siri Guru Granth Sahib
McCauliffe translation

Table of Contents

Dedication 2

Introduction 3

Stephen N. Xenakis, M.D. 4

HarSimran Kaur 6

Hersh Hernandez, USMC (ret.) 9

Preface 10

A Roadmap to Spiritual Growth 12

Death, Grief, Despair 15

The Horror 16

Grief 29

Family, Friends, and the "real" World 34

My Spouse 41

The Outside World Projecting In 43

Suicide 44

Death 47

New Understandings and A Glimmer of Light 48

Balls and Birds 49

My Fundamental Kernel of Truth 51

Reincarnation 53

Life Forms and Their Souls 56

Meaning and Purpose 58

The Practice.. 59

The Saint-Soldier... 62

I and You 64

Comfort Zones.. 66

The Invisible Worlds... 70

Synchronicity, Chaos Theory and Anti-Chaos........................ 78

God.. 79

The Tapestry... 81

Good and Evil 83

Good.. 88

Duality 90

The Human Experience 92

Sin and Karma 95

Body, Mind and Soul 97

Paradoxes 99

Countless worlds – Visible and Invisible............................. 101

Faith, Belief, Conviction and Knowledge 103

Destiny, Fate, Pre-Destination, and Free Will 107

Love 109

Forgiveness 111

Compassion 112

The Path... 113

The Three Pillars 115
The Five Thieves 117

Insights, Inspirations, Revelations 120
Many Paths 123
Governance and Miri-Piri 125
Illusion 127
Justice 129
Community 130
Hopes, Wishes, Desires and Expectations 133
Detachment 134
Truth 136
The Conduit 138
A Higher Consciousness 140
Purgatory 144
Heaven, Valhalla, Paradise 146
and the Realm of Truth 146
The Final Frontier 146
Nirvana 148
Melding with God 148
Epilogue 149

Dedication

In tribute and with love to my wife Barbara, my mother Helen, my sister-in-law Nancy; to my friends Mrs. Connie Dineen Hernandez, Terry Leary, Sharon Richardson, Joyce Swaney and Senora Josefina Parellado Morato; and to all other mothers who have lost a child.

Only mothers can know the full depth of life's greatest tragedy. The death of one conceived and carried within, born from their flesh into the world and nurtured thereafter, is a wound that will never heal.

Introduction

By way of an introduction, I have asked three friends from different life experiences to provide a few words from their perspectives on matters I write about in the following pages.

I have greatly valued their wisdom, honesty and friendship and am grateful for their contributions herein.

Stephen N. Xenakis, M.D.

Dr. Xenakis is an adult, child, and adolescent psychiatrist with many years of clinical, academic, and management experience. He retired from the U.S. Army in 1998 at the rank of brigadier general and entered an active career in start-up medical technologies and clinical practice. He has advised the Chairman of the Joint Chiefs of Staff and other senior Department of Defense officials on psychological health and the effects of blast concussion. During his career in the Army, he pioneered the introduction of telemedicine applications including the development of a device for electronic house call services. He has developed and promoted innovative and practical technology for the diagnosis and treatment of neuropsychiatric conditions. His most recent endeavor leverages the application of machine learning and predictive analytics to identifying individuals at risk for suicide, violence, and dangerous conduct. He has evaluated many accused terrorists, including detainees at Guantánamo. Dr. Xenakis has numerous medical publications. He is an Adjunct Professor at the Uniformed Services of Health Sciences of the military medical department and former Erik Erikson Scholar at the Austen Riggs Center. Dr. Xenakis is a graduate of Princeton University and the University of Maryland School of Medicine.

Michael Bajek is a deeply spiritual man searching for meaning in the shadow of his son's death. He conjures karma, ponders reincarnation, and is perplexed by the all-too-human detritus of his loss. He hunts for the soul in every corner of his life – his animals, the wildlife visiting his farm, and his most intimate loved ones. And, he struggles to make sense of the son's life that vanished all too quickly for him. In his quest, he has touched on the life quadrants of purpose and meaning, morality, and moral injury. Michael's son Kane served 2 combat tours as a Marine. He came home haunted by images of thoughtlessness and senseless killing. He was not afraid to kill the enemy or to die. But, he could not escape the images of innocent victims and the violence of war. Is it any surprise that his son, like so many young men and women, felt shock by seeing grandmothers and young children fall dead on the battlefield?

Michael's grief steered him to a religious life dedicated to God and commitment to a mission of standing up for truth, justice, freedom, sovereignty, and ethics in a worldly life. He found meaning, purpose, and a spiritual tradition for his life. Most importantly, the spiritual meaning he discovered blended his humanistic instincts and identity as a soldier.

Michael brings the reader along his path of grief and discovery about his son's life. He cannot fathom the mystery of his life, or the death that unsettled him, and he cannot escape the shattering impact on his life. He grew up as a Catholic and experienced God as a Being that loomed large and was unsettling. And so, he instinctively searched out other spiritual traditions and the essence he needed to comfort him and make sense of his deepest pains. The reader feels his moments of hazed consciousness and breakthrough light. Michael grasps at the myths and allegories, metaphors and poetry to describe creation and God. Michael's grief has inspired him to his personal search for God and meaning.

Not all readers will feel as Michael does, or identify with his sensibilities. His story flows out of his son's death, and his knowing that Kane could not escape profound moral injuries from his combat experiences. But, any of us who have been shocked by immense grief, horror, or confusion identify with his journey – even if it were not the one we would have taken – for it is all too human.

HarSimran Kaur

HarSimran Kaur is a young Sikh activist and educator. At the core, she is a healer (in training) and is involved with many organizations where she shares her passion for Gurbani, Social justice and Health care with people and serves this world fulfilling her own unique calling to heal, empower and support people, using many different natural and conventional medical therapies, but also Gurbani, Naam, meditation and chanting.

Healing as I see it, is the re-establishment of wholesomeness. If you ask yourself, perhaps every evening this week: Am I living a wholesome existence? You might find, that more likely than not, wholesomeness may not be your regular state of being.

The loss of one's child, a son or a daughter, I wonder, may be one of those losses that one may never completely heal from, completely forget and move on from, but this is not to say that one cannot, even if they truly want to, cope with it or healthily deal with it. This book, outlines Michael's journey towards coping with the loss of Kane, his son. The ideology and thoughts that he found solace and some fragments of wholesomeness in. I feel that this will serve you, in whatever way it is meant to. I invite you to dive into his journey, as he shares with you, what he found useful, comforting and soothing to his aching heart. I hope that you will find some healing comfort in his words.

Healing is re-establishment of wellness on a holistic level, an overall sense of mental, emotional, physical, financial and social well being, wholesomeness and harmony with one's life trajectory, circumstances and progression. One can find comfort in a multitude of things, distractions, activities, hobbies, etc. However, in the Sikh tradition, they say, healing can only be found in the Shabad. Shabad is many things, and yet it is a very specific entity. I would define Shabad as the vibrational frequency, the naad that you tune into, during meditation. "Shabad dhun naad" is an expression used to define Shabad in the Guru Granth Sahib Ji, the Sikh text of ultimate spiritual guidance, which literally translates to - the sound (or a perceivable expression) of the Shabad is naad- the vibratory force that is integral to every living or non-living being, like your heartbeat, like the waves of the ocean, like the brownian motion found in the subatomic particles of all things. In essence then, Naad is the connection to one's inner, most pure self. And therefore, when we silence the mind, meditate and focus our attention - whether it is on a spot on the wall in front of you or the sensations on the tip of your nose while your eyes are closed, or your heartbeat or your numinous, whatever it is, or a mantra, like Wa-hey-guru, the Sikh name for the essence that takes you from darkness to light- chanting it long enough, we dive deeper into the depths of our being and find the many 'gifts' as the Sikh tradition says reside within our beings. Some of which are undoubtedly peace, solace and comfort, which likely aren't found right away on the surface of course, but as one's practice continues, they are encountered relatively soon. At first, your time in meditation forces you to look at yourself in the mirror, sometimes we have to face the dark parts of ourselves before the encounters with peace occur. But as our meditation practice grows and deepens, we encounter peace and perhaps even bliss. Throughout the process, lots of letting go and surrendering occurs, wherein profound healing can happen. Of course that is just my peoples' belief, and I do not think that that's the ultimate or the only verdict on healing. But I do somehow feel that like my elders say, ultimate healing is only found within, and not without. You have to actively work towards it. And yes, sounds like too much work, but it happens rather quickly or at least with intuitive poise (Sehaj).

Regardless of what you find works for you, everyone's healing story is unique. Reading Michael's helped me deal with a recent loss of my own. And I hope that you find some comfort, some level of healing, or something of use, in this journey that is replete with Michael's personal truths, pain, struggle, ideas and thoughts in which he found comfort. I hope that you will find yourself embarking on a journey towards your own personal healing, as you read and experience Michael's.

ਨਾਮੁ ਨਿਧਾਨੁ ਸਤਿਗੁਰੂ ਸੁਣਾਇਆ ਮਿਟਿ ਗਏ ਸਗਲੇ ਰੋਗਾ ਜੀਉ

Nām niḏẖān saṯgurū suṇā▫i▫ā mit ga▫e sagle rogā jī▫o.
The True Guru has inspired me to hear the Treasure of the Naam; all my illness has been dispelled.

ਸਰਬ ਰੋਗ ਕਾ ਅਉਖਦੁ ਨਾਮੁ ॥

Sarab rog kā a▫ukẖaḏ nām.
The Naam is the panacea, the remedy to cure all ills.

ਕਲਿਆਣ ਰੂਪ ਮੰਗਲ ਗੁਣ ਗਾਮ ॥

Kali▫āṇ rūp mangal guṇ gām.
Singing the Glory of God is the embodiment of bliss and emancipation.

Hersh Hernandez, USMC (ret.)

Horacio "Hersh" Hernandez is a twenty year veteran of the United States Marine Corps. He retired as a Lieutenant Colonel. Since his retirement he has been overseeing contract security operations, for over twenty years, in several U S Embassies in Sub-Saharan Africa.

For those who are connected by this tragic experience, you must accept that grief will be a part of your life forever more. The grief will evolve, but you will have to decide to embrace those memories that bring joy, cherishing the time, however short, spent with your lost one, or to go into that dark place which only focuses on the loss. How you choose will determine the rest of your life.

May Mike's book help you choose to live life fully until you are reunited and there is only joy.

Preface

I am writing this book to describe a year and a half of utter emotional darkness; and to convey certain insights derived, even if just to one person in some small way, as a means of service. At the three year point, I am now just barely emerging from the pit, so this is not, and can never be, a complete tale.

I know there are many others who have also experienced the deep despair and dissolution of spirit following the death of one's child. Some emerge apparently intact, others never regain their strength, but in all cases I am certain such a personal tragedy was a life-changer, even if we as outsiders cannot see it. I hope that my experience will be of value to anyone suffering emotionally, whether from loss of a loved one or from a spiritual vacuum, whatever the cause. I hope that for those who are now in a good place, that this recounting of my own personal journey will in some way better prepare them for losses that they will inevitably endure in the future. Also, I hope this account will help family and friends of those suffering from an immediate loss to better understand what they are going through.

My approach will be from the perspective of a new religion, and new God. I had initially wanted to be as ecumenical and secular as possible and avoid any direct mention of any religion. However, this would not have been truthful on my part. I could not honestly portray my own journey without describing the religious dilemmas I faced. Only hard-hitting truth, from my perspective, can convey the black depths to which I sank and the glimmers of light which drew me back to a more secure consciousness. Please understand that while I begin this account terribly angry, and my language will certainly be offensive to many, this book does not end that way. I bear no enmity towards any person or group, any religion or philosophy and have the utmost respect for those who follow their own faith in good conscience. And I feel compassion for those who struggle, as I have and still do, to understand the great questions of life.

I had thought I would not bring in stories of real persons, particularly those close to me. However, interactions with people are inevitable, even during times of grief. Some encounters are helpful, some cause pain, anger and anguish. Herein, I will start with anger, despair, hopelessness, and end, even in a small proportion, with a sense of compassion, regeneration, and understanding.

A Roadmap to Spiritual Growth

Rather than leave a summary and my conclusions to the end, I prefer to begin with them. The reason is that I fully understand a good many people who would read this book are looking for answers and a way forward during times of great stress. They may very well be unable to bear wading through to the end and thus would miss what I feel are some very basic steps that anyone, regardless of religious beliefs or circumstances, can take to assume a new spiritual direction that will help them overcome whatever inner turmoil they are facing.

So here goes.

Reach deep down into your innermost being, your very self, your soul, and find your most strongly held truth. Forget what your religion tells you to believe or your family, friends and community believe. What is the most basic truth you know? You will have at least one strong conviction about life, death, and the nature of creation. You may have many beliefs or tenets of faith, but be truthful with yourself. If you come up with too many, you may well be reciting theological dogma that originates with others. What do you, yourself, know in your deepest inner soul is true? Take this truth and hold it dear, cherish and protect it. This is the foundation of all other truths that build up the structure or your world view. It is yours alone. No one can ever take it away from you. There are no penalties.

How do you grow, protect, and fully derive comfort from your truth and collection of truths? You need a path, a direction, a way to follow that will allow your faith to continuously be a creative and positive influence in your life. The easiest route would be to adhere more vigorously to the religion you have followed in the past. Much will have already been learned and can be built on. But you may no longer find your old religion a comfort. Possibly there is another congregation or denomination of the same religion that you would find more satisfying. Possibly you may want to change religions, each of which will have many different groupings and denominations. Possibly you may want to meld several denominations or even several religions into your own hybrid religion. Possibly you may want to create your very own religion from scratch. Whatever your answer might be, it is imperative to discover an existing or to create a brand new religious system that will accommodate your viewpoint as you have identified it. Be aware that there may be penalties if your viewpoint deviates from the dogma of the established religious grouping you currently belong to or that you would like to join. Be true to yourself and the truths you have identified. Your path, like your truths, must be your very own if it is to have value.

Formulate a practice that will strengthen and solidify your foundation of truth and your religion. A practice that does not take place often is unlikely to be of much good. A practice that includes at least one daily spiritual undertaking, even if just a short period of meditation or prayer, is just about essential. The conscious soul, when awake, and the unconscious soul when asleep need to be nurtured. They need to be fed.

Live a healthy, productive, moral, compassionate, just and honest life. God focus, purity of soul cannot be sustained in a life of pride, greed, anger, carnality and undisciplined love of the physical world.

Live and participate in a community that shares at least some elements of your set of truths, your chosen religion and your moral and spiritual values. You will derive comfort, insights, and wisdom from frequent interaction with those sharing a commonality of purpose and meaning. But be tolerant of those who are of other religions, nationalities, races or gender. Treat all life forms with love and respect.

Give selfless service – service to your community will come most naturally, but do not forget wider humanity and most especially those who have greater needs than you, wherever they might be.

Strive to be a Soldier-Saint and cross this terrible world-ocean.

**Death
Grief
Despair**

The Horror

On April 8, 2013, I received an email message from a young Liberian friend in Monrovia, Liberia that set in motion a total upheaval of my existence as I had known it. She said that she was very worried about my son Kane who had been living there for the past five months. The message said that he was constantly being admitted to a local clinic for treatment, had lost a great deal of weight and didn't appear to be taking care of himself; that he had made some new friends who she felt were bad people, and that she felt I should bring him back home to the US as soon as possible. A coldness, a fear gripped me upon reading that message. I tried to reach my son by telephone that night with no success. I tried again the next morning and his phone was answered by a Liberian man who said he was Kane's friend; that he had brought Kane to the clinic the previous night, and the night before; that Kane was receiving blood transfusion and that he, the friend was going to visit him that moment. I asked him to get the doctor's phone number as soon as he arrived at the clinic, and I would call to get it in a half hour. I got the number and then called the doctor who said that Kane had received two pints of blood and needed two more. The doctor said he was funding the treatment out of his own pocket and that Kane now owed him $1,000. I told the doctor I would send the money immediately, to do all that was necessary and that money was not a problem. I then asked the doctor if I should bring Kane home immediately. He said "Sure, if he makes it." My blood ran cold. I told him to do everything necessary to treat him, hung up, and immediately called my Liberian friends, and one of my best friends in the world, a Lebanese businessman – Jean known by most as "JJ", and begged them to immediately get Kane to one of the two best hospitals in the city.

I prayed to God the Father and Jesus with all my heart, mind and soul. Never in my life had I so totally put my whole being and substance into prayer. I was terribly afraid.

Over the next several hours my friends gave me frequent updates. They had put their full energies into getting Kane into the hospital where he would receive the best treatment. They had given their personal guarantees of payment to the hospital that agreed to admit. My Liberian friends picked Kane up from the Stockton Creek Clinic in their 4x4 Toyota and brought him to John F. Kennedy Hospital, arriving at close to midnight. The doctor on duty was a personal friend, former classmate of my friend Thomatta, educated abroad, a competent doctor, and he guaranteed to her that he would give Kane everything necessary to get well. He said Kane would recover. Kane was semi-comatose, in great pain and struggling. He had to be strapped to a gurney in order to get intravenous needles in him and then was wheeled to the intensive care unit. Thomatta and her husband James then left for home, and she called me from the car to tell me Kane would be fine and was under good care.

With all my heart, mind and soul, I thanked God the Father and Jesus for this blessing, tears were running down my face. I was so relieved. I truly believed this was a divine intervention. I had faith.

Two hours later I received a text message from Thomatta that read: "Mike, the doctor just called. Kane didn't make it."

Kane died at 2:30 AM, Monrovia time, on April 10, my 58th birthday. He was just short of his 29th.

Empty – that is the only way to describe how I felt at that moment. The life force had been sucked out. I went to my wife Barbara, put my arms around her and said, "Baby, Kane's dead. He just died". And then I wailed. I did not cry, I can see myself now in memory as another person. I wailed like an animal who has been trapped, tortured, and knows it is going to die, a primeval sound of utter despair. I was soon filled with a cascading rush of strong emotions. I felt abandoned, betrayed, cruelly attacked, lied to, tricked by God the Father and Jesus and the whole fucking world. I was then overcome by bitter hatred and rage. I started chanting over and over: "God is evil, Jesus is evil; fuck God and fuck Jesus." They were my mortal enemies and if I had to spend the rest of this life and countless future lives battling these monstrosities I would. I chanted this mantra for days, particularly at night because I couldn't sleep. My wife would scream at me to stop, and I would stop for awhile, but would then just wail.

The night he died I stayed up and called everyone I needed to: I first called Jean, my Lebanese friend in Monrovia. He was shocked to the core. I asked him first to get Kane's body to a funeral home and embalmed, but then to make arrangements with the Indian Sikh community for a traditional cremation. I also asked him to immediately find and take care of Kane's little dog Rambo. Rambo had wandered onto our farm at six months old, feral all his life and sick. Kane took care of him and the two were strongly bonded. Kane took him with him to Liberia and I knew that without Kane, Rambo would not survive the day. Liberians eat dogs. I then called Kane's older brother Aaron, the eldest; my then 88 year old mother, and Barbara's two sisters and brother.

Much of the following week was a blur. One of Barbara's sisters came up from Atlanta within 24 hours to stay with her. I brought down from Philadelphia a Liberian man, who I had brought to the US to help on the farm, a good friend of Kane's. He had moved to Philadelphia after four years with us because we were no longer in a position to support him and his wife and two children. But he had immediately agreed to return to take care of our horses and property knowing that Barbara couldn't do it while I went to Liberia. Our son Aaron and his pregnant wife had come down the day after Kane died, and he returned daily for two weeks to be with his mom. Making sure Barbara was looked after, plus travel arrangements, getting a visa, meant I didn't arrive in Monrovia until one week after Kane's death. My friend Jean had promised me he would do everything possible to keep the funeral home generators running 24/7, there is no public power in Monrovia. That said, generators and coolers fail so there was no guarantee that Kane's body could be preserved. Thus the necessity to have cremation preparations on standby for immediate need. In tropical West Africa, bodies decompose rapidly. My other very closest friend there, a Spanish engineer at the Firestone Rubber Plantation, had lost his brother in a car accident in a remote area of Ghana 10 years earlier. It took my friend three days to get to the site and by then his brother was so decomposed as to be unrecognizable, and un-embalmable for transport to Spain for the funeral his mother wanted. He was cremated in Accra, in traditional Sikh fashion, just as I was arranging for Kane.

Flights and airport times took 28 hours before I reached Monrovia. I remember none of them. My Spanish friend Raimon and Jordanian friend Lillian picked me up at the airport and brought me back to his house on the plantation, 40 miles from Monrovia. My friends were exceedingly kind and it meant a great deal for me to be with them. They had taken great care of Kane when he first arrived in Liberia and had included them in their group of closest friends, the deep sea fishing club that was also very important to me during the five years I lived there. Jean sent a car for me the next day to bring me to his house, where I stayed for the next two weeks. He and my other friends couldn't have been more compassionate or solicitous. Jean had taken care of all the legal and administrative needs with government, paid the funeral home in advance and even provided them daily diesel fuel to keep the generators operating. I was housed, fed, transported and never left alone. My son's dog Rambo was at Jean's house when I arrived. He didn't recognize me and looked so, so sad. At night he was let off his leash and would follow Jean's old security guard around his patrols of the property, never leaving his side.

On the third day, in the morning, I went to see Kane's body. The funeral home prepared him in advance and had him on a gurney under a white sheet in the chapel. I went over to him and touched his hand, then his cheek, then kissed his forehead. Cold, cold, cold, unmoving, dead. He looked like he could have woken up at that moment. But he didn't. He was dead. Then I really cried. I almost collapsed and the funeral director and my driver supported me over to a pew, where I sat, face buried in hands. And cried.

In the afternoon, I went to the American Embassy to process the official Report of Death Abroad, the official US death certificate. The Deputy Chief of Mission, who I had known for 28 years, and the Ambassador's secretary who I had known for 22, came down to the Consular Section to see me and express their condolences. I appreciated this, but found it odd that they couldn't come out from behind the bullet proof window to shake hands. We touched fingers through the document tray.

I then went to see my two retired Marine friends, who ran the large US Embassy and UN guard force contracts. I had known them since the civil war days and I had trusted and counted on them without question during my tours in Monrovia. They didn't recognize me. During four years of retirement in rural Virginia my hair and beard had grown long and turned very white. Once Hersh, the retired Marine Force Recon Colonel, recognized me we had a laugh, until I told him that he and I were now members of a very unhappy club. Hersh had lost his 24 year old daughter to cancer seven years before. Hersh had been through "secret" wars as an active Marine and badly wounded. He had also lived through much of the Liberian civil war. All put together this man had seen more death and misery than anyone I know. But, even tough guys shed tears as he did that day when he gave me a bear hug.

When I left Hersh and Tony, I went straight to Jean's barber, had him shave my beard completely and cut my hair very short. The barber and his friends in the shop, all Lebanese who I had never met, showed tremendous compassion and sympathy to me, a stranger, when I told them why I was there.

On the fourth day, I went to meet my old friend of 16 years, the Indian Honorary Consul General. An ethnic Punjabi and devotee of the Sikh religion, Jeety is one of the wealthiest businessmen in Liberia. He is also the patriarch of the Indian community of 2,000 so his consular position, while honorary and unpaid is also real work as he issues visas, performs notary services, and functions as the de facto Indian diplomatic representative. That day he broke off from his business and official duties and we drove to the crematorium, 30 miles outside the city on the road to the Firestone plantation. He had constructed and paid for the crematorium himself, as a service to the community, but had not visited it in a year. Liberians do not believe in cremations and a year earlier had raised an uproar, accusing the Indians of "roasting and eating human flesh". Kane's cremation would be the first test of whether that sentiment still prevailed and Jetty was confident that my status as a retired senior diplomat who had served two tours during Liberia's civil war, and Kane's status as a former US Marine, would mute any public criticism.

The five acre crematorium compound was overgrown with brush and trees – one year of neglect in the tropics assured this. The fifteen foot iron gate had been torn off its hinges and lay a few feet outside the gateway – thieves had attempted to carry it away but it was too heavy. Jeety immediately told his staff to hire workers from the village to clear the brush and clean the compound, sent out workmen to remount the gate, and put 24 hour guards on the property. When Jeety and I walked out, joining my friend Jean at the vehicles, Jeety pointed to the crematorium and said "Michael, this is the one truth we all share."

This was my first insight into the Sikh religion.

Kane's funeral and cremation took place on Saturday, April 21 at the Saint Moses Funeral Home. His body was laid out in a fancy bronze casket. The bottom half was closed and covered by the American flag folded in half. He was dressed in a black suit and tie. I had brought his first official photo as a Marine when he was 18 years old and it was mounted on a stand nearby. Close to 50 of my friends attended. I counted 11 nationalities among them. Only four were American - myself, the two Marines conducting military honors in dress blue uniforms, and Tony my long time friend, a retired Marine Sergeant Major. There were Christians of various denominations, Muslims, Hindus, Sikhs, Druze and followers of native African religions. Everyone passed by the casket for the viewing, some touched his hands, some made the sign of the cross, some cried. After everyone was seated the funeral director closed the casket and the Marines unfolded the flag to cover the entire casket.

The funeral director, an evangelical Christian Minister, led prayers. The organist played hymns. I read a family eulogy, which I had written out the night before, so that if I broke down my friend Jean could finish for me. I made it through ok. Jean said a few words, other people who knew Kane spoke, my Liberian former secretary, who had sponsored Kane when he arrived and taken him to the hospital the day he died, gave condolences on behalf of the US Embassy. Only four of the local staff were there and no Americans from the State Department, my career agency for 25 years. Apparently the Ambassador had a command performance activity for the entire staff. I had expected many of the 200 Liberian embassy employees to attend, but I understood the choice was not theirs. The Ambassador, I thought at the time, might have delayed her event an hour so that staff could attend the funeral service. None of Kane's new supposed friends were there. People later told me that even months later they had disappeared from the community where he lived.

The Marines, in a time honored ritual, removed the flag from the casket and, one at each end, ceremonially folded the flag into a triangle. The Major presented the flag to me, expressing the thanks of the President of the United States, the Secretary of Defense, the US Marines, and a grateful nation for my son's service. The mournful bugle call "Taps" was played. I later saw in the video, that my Marine friend Tony was wiping his eyes. I am sure that this was the first time my friends of many nationalities had seen such an impressive formal presentation of military honors to a dead comrade in arms. The US Marines are especially revered in Liberia, where they have many times been a protective force during the long civil war.

The ceremony over, the casket was wheeled out and somewhere in the back of the funeral home Kane was transferred into a simple wooden casket and into the back of the hearse – a heavy duty, 4x4 Toyota Land Cruiser. The Chief of Police had provided a police escort. At the chapel exit I greeted and hugged each and every one of the people who attended. Only a small number of my closest friends were to attend the cremation, along with about thirty family and associates of my Sikh friend Jeety, who assisted in the cremation. The crematorium had been cleared and cleaned up as Jeety said it would. The concrete platform in the center was piled with wood. Six Sikh men, all impressive figures in their turbans and long black beards, carried the coffin from the hearse and laid it on the pyre. The lid was opened, Kane exposed once more to view, the traditional Sikh way. They wrapped his face in cotton, then poured liquid ghee, rarefied butter, all over the cotton and around his body. All of us in attendance placed incense sticks all over him and around the inside of the coffin. The Sikhs and myself, barefoot and heads covered, all gathered at the head of the coffin, with me in the center, and sang Ardas, the beautiful prayer sung at all important events - weddings, births, and cremations – as well as by each individual Sikh in the morning and evening.

My friend Jeety then handed me a pole, the tip of which was wrapped in cotton and soaked in ghee. The torch was then lit. I then went around the pyre, lighting the wood on every side. We then all stood back and watched the fire grow hotter and higher.

At one point, one of the Sikhs responsible for the fire, who would stay on through the night, came over to me and drew my attention to the fact that Kane's head was not burning. He would have to add more wood there. But first, he took a long pole and smashed in Kane's skull. It is the Sikh tradition that this be done to set the soul free.

We stayed for no more than two hours. There was nothing more for us to do. Several Sikhs stayed through the night and added more wood. The site was guarded around the clock for three days to prevent intrusion. On the third day Jeety, Jean, several Sikhs and myself returned, as the fire was now cold. We covered our heads, removed our shoes and socks and went onto the cremation platform. We picked through the ashes to find all of Kane's bones that had not been consumed by the fire, even tiny fragments. We washed these in a bucket filled with water and yoghurt as was traditional. I then took all the bones, about five pounds worth, and put them in plastic bags and then into a temporary plastic cremation urn approved for international travel. This is what I brought back to Kane's mother. All of the rest of the ashes we swept up and put into three empty rice sacks, about 150 pounds of the remains of wood, clothes, coffin, butter and of course ashes of Kane. The water and yoghurt solution I later poured into Monrovia's

Saint Paul River. The following weekend, my fishing buddies and I took the ashes and spread them on the water 12 miles out into the Atlantic Ocean.

I felt good about the funeral and cremation. It had a taste of the ecumenical and international. Most important, with the Marines and Sikhs, both of noted martial traditions, it had the taste of a warrior tribute. And spreading the ashes at sea reminded me of the Viking tradition. Kane would have liked it, and probably also would have gotten a real kick out of the all terrain hearse.

I had had the funeral ceremonies and cremation filmed, and brought the recording back so that Kane's mother, along with family and friends, could see him one last time and see that we tried our very best to give him the most dignified and respectful send off possible.

The following week in Monrovia was spent clearing up remaining business. I wanted to go to the house Kane had rented, both to see it and to see what of his personal belongs remained and what I might want to bring back. It was a small two bedroom one bath house, and like most Liberian housing without electricity and running water. Water would be trucked in to fill 55 gallon plastic barrels. Electricity, for those who could afford them, came from small portable generators, usually just enough to run a few light bulbs and a television for several hours a day. All of Kane's personal belongings were gone. Just a few old tee shirts and short pants remained in the house. He had gone out there with an expensive mountain bike, computer tablet, digital camera, and nice portable stereo system. All were apparently stolen when he was sick in the clinic. He had also told me he had bought a small motorcycle. No one knew anything about it. Just before leaving the area, someone from the community came running up. He had Kane's camouflage floppy hat from his Marine days, one of his treasured mementos. Written in pen on the inside was "March 22, 2003 Kuwait March 23, 2003 Iraq. This was the cap he wore during the invasion of Iraq. It was the only thing of his I returned with.

I then went to see Thomatta and James, the Liberian friends of mine who had taken care of Kane when he first arrived in Monrovia. I asked about his last few hours and they told me he had been in great pain and kept telling them not to touch him when they were taking him to the hospital. I asked if he had said anything that would be of any meaning to me or his mother. James said that the very last time they saw him, when he was strapped to the gurney and being wheeled down the hall to the intensive care unit, he kept on yelling out "Dad, Dad, Daddy, Daddy", then went silent.

His maid, who had remained behind to stay with him during the night, was not in the room when he died. He died alone, without family or friends. I paid her the $30 monthly wage that Kane owed her.

Before I left Monrovia, I went to see the doctor, the friend of Thomatta's who had treated him at the end at John F. Kennedy Hospital. He was a very nice and compassionate young man, very intelligent, and he obviously felt terrible that he couldn't save Kane. He said if he had gotten him even hours earlier he could have turned things around. He said the doctor and the Stockton Creek Clinic had not been treating his malaria aggressively enough and that he also had a high bacteria count which is why he had noted on his death certificate that he had died of cardiac arrest and septicemia. He said towards the very end Kane stopped blinking and his neck went rigid, his heartbeat soared to 156 beats per minute and it was evident that the malaria had gone cerebral, the parasites were into the brain.

I also stopped by Catholic Hospital, which had refused to admit Kane earlier in the day due to a previous unpaid bill. I paid the $79 debt.

I passed by the Stockton Creek Clinic, but did not go in. I did not search out the doctor there who could have saved Kane, but who kept him sick in order to keep sucking money out of him. I did not search out his new friends, who knowing he was sick could have let some of my affluent, older friends know and let them get him proper treatment, but preferred to steal his belongings when he was dying. I had wanted to kill all of them, including the doctor, but by now I was so weak and deadened and uncaring I let it go. I still carry the hunting knife with me all my waking hours, whether in a suit or shorts. But now, to me, it represents my obligation to pursue justice for all, not vengeance. I have no doubt those people will get their due sometime somewhere.

Several days before leaving Monrovia, I made the arrangements for Rambo to return with me. We were now quite bonded. He had discovered that small green mangos fell from the trees at Jean's house. I started throwing them to him – this clicked with him as the mangos looked similar enough to tennis balls to remind him of the great fun he and Kane had throwing and chasing them.

I remember very little of my arrival back in the US. I do remember that I was consumed with finding an answer to why Kane had come to such a bitter end. And why Barbara and my lives had been shredded so brutally. I saw only two choices for me: one, believe in an evil God the Father and an evil Jesus and fight them in the hopes of battling to a better reality beyond them; or I could decide not to believe in them. I chose the latter option.

I de-created God the Father and Jesus. Poof, they ceased to exist. I felt a heavy weight lift from me. What is the point in hating and fighting something that does not exist? Freedom. It felt like real freedom to be rid of them.

But then I felt an emptiness too. If they did not exist, what of importance was there? If we are just a soup of chemicals and minerals somehow combined into a life form what is the point in that? Who cares? If life didn't really suck maybe I would think it was something special and want to survive as long as I could to appreciate every little bit of goodness life offered. But, life does suck. There is more pain and suffering than there is pleasure and happiness, so why keep flogging this dead horse? Why bother?

I did want to find something that made sense, that instilled meaning and purpose into what from my perspective was a shitty existence. So I started re-visiting a lot of my old studies into religion, philosophy, quantum physics, anthropology, history, paleontology, and the occult. Not in-depth re-reading of the great works of history, but a quick perusal to see what I should still reject and what I might still want to hold onto. What concepts did I believe in the past, what did I still believe? What new concepts could I discover that would fill that cold empty space of no meaning, purpose, or value?

Grief

Traditional grief therapy and counseling has relied on a five stage process through which the individual must pass following the death of a loved one. The five stages roughly follow this pattern. These stages may very well prove true for some, but they did not for me.

Denial — The loss being hard to face, the person shuts out the reality and develops a false, preferable reality. My initial, microsecond reaction was disbelief, followed almost immediately by shock and a profound emotional, mental anguish.

Anger — the five stage theory states that the individual recognizes that denial cannot continue and anger follows – anger with himself, others, or at a higher power. This theory speaks of the anger being misplaced, making it hard for others to take care of them. For me, anger was simultaneous with disbelief and anguish. The anger was directed at God the Father and Jesus. This anger ended once I de-created them. Anger against those close to me did take place quite later and lasted far longer, but it was not misplaced. I became angry because of specific insensitive actions they initiated. Was my anger appropriate and balancing the insensitivities against the far greater kindnesses they showed? No, it was far too elevated, rejectionist and corrosive to my inner self. My anger ended suddenly one day as I will explain later.

Bargaining — The traditional stage involves the hope that the individual can somehow undo or avoid a cause of grief. I never experienced this stage. I knew the truth from the very moment I received the news. What I did do is try to relive every moment of my son's life, particularly the last few years, and most especially the last few weeks, trying to think of what I could have done to prevent his death. I blamed myself for every course of action taken or not taken that might have led to his death. This period lasted for a long while, and to be honest still does today.

Depression — During the fourth stage of the counseling model, the grieving person begins to understand the certainty of death and the idea of living becomes pointless. The grieving person disconnects from love and affection, feels sadness, regret, fear, and uncertainty when going through this stage, and the traditional model sees this as positive, a beginning of acceptance and closure. I did feel a deep sadness and everything to me was uncertain. However, while not knowing the point to life, I felt there must be.

Acceptance — In this last stage, individuals come to terms with the loss of a loved one, or other tragic event and, according to the model, typically develops a calm, retrospective view and a stable mindset. From the beginning, I rejected the concept of acceptance or closure. To me, acceptance denotes a degree of approval while closure signals the time has come to move on, be normal, return to status quo. While I have sought an understanding, and continue to seek meaning, I very much doubt I will ever accept my son's death. I am not the same person I was before. The key question was whether I would or could use this life-changing event to become a better wiser human being, or whether I would let myself be permanently and irrevocably overcome by it.

Remember, this is your grief, taking place in the deepest part of you – your soul. Do not let anyone tell you how to grieve, how you will grieve, what stages are natural and inevitable and which ones are inappropriate. Do not let anyone tell you how long to grieve and when it is time to buck up and move on. Unless you really want to, do not feel obliged to resume your regular activities – whether work related or recreational. Being around people too is not necessarily therapeutic, even people you love. Protect yourself. Guard against intrusions that may only make matters worse for you. Say no if that is your gut feeling, even if other feelings are hurt. Recognize that you are a new person, even if you and others still want you want to be the person you were before.

Grief, in a medical sense, should be classified as Post-Traumatic Stress Disorder, or PTSD. It isn't. The orthodox psychiatric definition, still rigidly adhered to is that PTSD is the emotional trauma produced by an actual life-threatening incident – a car accident, a rape, combat. The definition insists that there must be a fear for one's own life or for those one is intimately close to, in an actual physical incident where one is present. I strongly believe there are many other situations with high emotional impact that can be just as powerfully debilitating as to fall under the broad heading of PTSD. I think if a broader optic on the origins of emotional distress was recognized by the medical community there very well might be better success in treatment. PTSD is currently one of the most difficult mental problems to treat even when diagnosed according to the current medical definition. In many cases treatment is completely unsuccessful, because, I believe, the elemental problem goes far deeper than just fear for one's life.

I know a great deal about PTSD. A long time ago, I was treated for four years for severe depression by a highly respected psychiatrist, but with no success. My problem only got worse as more and more drugs were added to the cocktail, up to maximum dosages. The doctor had made it clear, and I agreed completely, that I was not psychotic, schizophrenic, bipolar, obsessive-compulsive, alcoholic or any of the host of other mental disorders. I had depression that did not respond to treatment. Unhappy with being a virtual zombie on drugs which were not helping, I had an insight one day, and told the psychiatrist that I believed I was suffering PTSD for an emotional, not physical, loss of 25 years before. I could tell this was a "eureka" moment for him. He worked closely with me and over the next six months I withdrew from the drugs, with great difficulty, but once drug free felt immensely better and was able to address my matter on my own.

My son Kane suffered terribly from PTSD after two combat tours in Iraq, having been involved in some of the heaviest fighting of the war. He did not respond to treatment and I believe now, following his death, that his PTSD did not relate to the traditional definition. He, like his fellow Marines, did not fear their own deaths. As one Marine, senior to my son in his unit, described these 18 and 19 year olds: "they were invincible, they had no fear, they were unstoppable". Kane, after his returns from Iraq, never expressed a fear of his own death. He did express deep grief for the Marine buddies who were killed, but I feel it was genuine sadness, and an honoring of their memory and lives rather than something that traumatized him. However, there are three incidents that make me think his trauma was related to something quite different, that deeply wounded his soul. He told me a story of his unit stopping in a small village as the Marines fought their way from Kuwait to Baghdad in the invasion. An old woman, dressed in black, her head covered in a black shawl, approached their tactical vehicles. She had a small woven basket in her hands covered with a cloth. The Marines yelled at her to get back. She did not understand and kept coming. The men in the adjoining vehicle shot her dead. When they uncovered the basket inside was a loaf of bread. She had wanted to give them a gift. I could tell this event affected Kane deeply. The second sign to me of something different going on was that he brought back only one war trophy – a children's illustrated book of Bible stories in Arabic. He refused to talk about it, but he kept it with his special treasures. The third glimpse I had into his mind was following another one of his sleepless nights, when he told me in a pitiful, anguished voice of another wartime horror that tormented him; one which even in my effort to be truthful in this writing I cannot repeat here.

Kane was not afraid for his own life. He was not afraid to kill other combatants, as that is the nature and understanding of war. But the death of innocents and the cruelty of war violated his humanity and wounded him deeply. His soul was bleeding. This is what killed him, not the malaria parasites in the body.

My imperfect, wonderful little boy bled to death from his soul.

Family, Friends, and the "real" World

"When you most need them your family will not be there. Your wife will see you and cry "Ghost, Ghost" and run away."

Siri Guru Granth Sahib
Sant Singh Khalsa translation

My mind was tormented. My body weak. The world surreally bleak and lifeless. I was very grateful for the compassion and many kindnesses of my friends in Monrovia. They showed me immeasurable respect and care. Their sadness for Kane was unquestionably genuine. Other friends of mine around the world and the US, and friends of Kane around the US asked for a copy of the funeral video. I sent out 30 videos which were then passed around to others and I figure at least 200 people saw it. One Italian friend in Rome, after watching the video, wrote me that he had viewed the whole thing, through the cremation, and just cried and cried and then went to his Catholic Church, lit candles and prayed. I had posted the news of his death on Kane's own Facebook page and received an outpouring of grief from his friends. Over the next several months many of his friends reached out to me and I saw a side of Kane that I hadn't seen before – he was liked, loved, and valued by so many. I was glad. It helped me knowing that he had made a positive impact on others.

I posted the news of his death on the webpage of his Marine unit – 1st Battalion, 4th Marine Regiment. Within 12 hours over 30 Marines posted responses, many who had fought with him in Iraq, including those both senior to him and those to whom he was senior – as a 20 year old corporal to 18 year old privates. I received messages from senior

Marines in the Regiment who had not even known Kane. To them a Marine was a Marine and they did care.

Our equine veterinarian, Todd, suffering himself as his wife was declining with breast cancer, spent hours with me discussing many of the life and death concepts contained in this book. Ricky, who has delivered our sawdust and gravel for 20 years, also spent long periods of time talking with me and giving me his "salt of the earth" perceptions.

Experience with closest family was in some instances wonderful, in others very troubling.

My mother, then 88, became my closest friend and most intimate confidant. I had never regarded her in those terms before. She was the only one I could pour my heart out to and she always listened. My only brother was deeply affected by Kane's death and my long-held opinion of him as a superficial person proved invalid. Both my mother and brother came up to visit us in Virginia from Alabama for three weeks shortly after my return from Monrovia. It was only with them that my wife, Barbara, one month after the funeral was able to bring herself to watch the video.

My nephew, two years older than Kane, to whom I had sent a video at my brother's request, never watched it. When I called him out on it I received a peevish, sarcastic response. His sister, my niece two years younger than Kane, sent a nice little phone text message of condolence, but not even a call or a card.

Barbara's family's response was most upsetting to me, though strange to me it didn't bother her. The sister closest in age, three years older, who had always been her best friend and idol, called the day after Kane's death. Barbara, when telling me about the call, was puzzled, confused – she was too much in shock then to feel hurt or more. She said her sister had made light of his death, even made jokes about it. For me, this was the start of an intense bitterness and anger towards anyone who I thought was not paying Kane the respect he deserved.

Her brother called and was kind, matter of fact, but it seemed to me, not as caring and compassionate to his sister as he should have been by maintaining contact with her over the days, weeks, and months that followed.

Barbara's oldest sister, the oldest sibling, came up to stay with Barbara from Atlanta within 24 of his death. Basically, she got in the car at first light the next day and drove the straight 11 hours here. She stayed a week and was extraordinarily caring and selfless. This was the person I most expected to be able to give me, myself personally, some sort of spiritual solace. She had lost her own son, a toddler, twenty plus years before; and then in subsequent years faced other personal tragedies through which she demonstrated tremendous courage and grace. She had turned deeply into religion and church community for strength. I never asked her for guidance in my grief, but she obviously would have known I was deeply troubled from the voicemail I had left the night Kane died – "Kane just died, god is evil, Jesus is evil, fuck them both." After my return from Monrovia, I received an email from her, forwarding an email from a friend of hers offering his insights in an effort to help me. After a recount of his experience with friends who had lost children, the message said "The Lord would not put more on your table than it can bear." My immediate thought was: "What sort of god would defecate on your table to the point it can bear no more, and then tell you to eat shit". My answer: an evil god.

I then read to the end of the email. People too often forward emails forgetting that their original emails to someone are also carried forward. After exuding much enthusiasm about the cruise they were about to take, my sister in law had written her friend that our son had died, that I was having trouble in my relationship with God, and that they were concerned about me because I was ranting and raving. Evidently a reference to the voicemail I left. What was I supposed to have said "Praise the Lord, my son is dead"? She then went on to say in her email to her friend that it was very possible that my son had wanted to die. Cold fury on my part at this point. How dare she make such a speculation under any circumstances? Kane's last words were calling for his daddy, for me to help. He did not want to die. And I wasn't there. I had not had his back and he died.

This was my final straw with hoping that the Christianity of my upbringing had any value for me.

Our only other son, Kane's eldest brother by four years, had been wonderful after receiving the news that night. He and his wife, five months pregnant with their first child, had come out immediately. My son arranged for and paid for my trip to Monrovia, gave me cash for the trip, drove me to the Liberian Embassy for the visa and then to the airport. He took a week off to spend every day with his mother who was not leaving her bed or eating during that time. He picked me and Rambo up from the airport upon return. He sent out the money to reimburse my friends in Monrovia for all the expenses – embalming, cold storage, funeral.

We did not see my son or his wife for three months after this, until their child, our first and probably only grandchild, was born on August 22, 2013. Her due date was actually August 18, which would have been Kane's 29th birthday. I was hoping the baby would be born that day so I could wonder if possibly this would be his reincarnation. I know my thinking was not rational; I just so much wanted to hold on to my son.

We visited the hospital after the baby was born and told them we would like to come see them after they got home, were settled in to the new baby routine, and ready for us. One month later we had not been invited to come. We were aware, since Barbara had spoken to our son, that they had

had almost daily visits from our daughter in law's aunts, uncles, cousins and friends. We were aware that she, being Korean, could receive too much attention from the extended family and we had not wanted to be part of the burden. But after one month Barbara decided we needed to pay a short visit. She called our son, who rarely answers his phone, and left a voicemail that we would like to come visit Sunday, five days away.

Three days later he calls back while commuting home from work. Barbara's eyes lit up, she had decided that being a grandmother was a nice thing. It was the only thing at that time that gave her any sense of the world being ok and that happiness and love were still possible. I watched her as she listened on the phone. The color drained from her face. Her cheeks and skin drooped. Her eyes went dull. Life drained out of her. There is nothing so horrifying as seeing life sucked out of a living person and have them still very much alive. I have seen people die and life pass away and then they are dead. My wife was still alive, but with no hope, no happiness, no reason for living.

My son had told her that we could come visit, but that we were to make it short, not to make it a big deal for his wife and stress her out. He wanted us to shower, put on clean clothes, and not smoke cigarettes in the car on the way up or while we were at their house (we never did smoke inside their house, but would go on the porch). Essentially he told Barbara we were dirty (we live on a farm with dogs, cats and horses) and unhealthy for the child.

Immediately after she told me this I was so indescribably angry. Our only remaining child, five months after the death of his only sibling, had attacked his mother in a way so cruel as to be unimaginable. I tried to call him back. He didn't answer although I knew he was still on his commute and knew I was calling. He had the courage to shatter his mother's love and hopes but not enough balls to face me. I left him a voicemail: an ugly, vile, obscenity riddled message. I had never in my life spoken to anyone like that. I hung up and told Barbara: "Both of my sons are now dead". She started to cry and said: "Please don't say that." I had never before in Aaron's whole life, 33 years at this point, spoken a harsh or angry word to him. He had always been the pride of my life, intelligent, kind, thoughtful, active, attentive to the welfare of his parents and his brother from a very early age. I was once again shattered.

Somehow she rebounded, and did speak to him. I wouldn't. Of all the people I had sent the video of the funeral to he was the only one who still had not bothered to watch it. When his mother first asked him several months after Kane's death he had said that he still found it too hard. The second time she asked, he asked why I had had to have the funeral over there. The third time, when Barbara and he were trying to repair the damage, and get us to visit for the granddaughter's 100th day birthday, a Korean tradition, he had said "that is really weird taking a video of a funeral" and asked whether this was the deal breaker on getting over the rupture with me, which Barbara said it was. Several days later he called and told her that he, his wife, and mother in law – who had come to stay with them for three months, had watched the video. I called him the next day and he said he had watched it and that the Marine ceremony was very nice. I didn't comment, but to this day I know in my heart of hearts that they did not watch the video of the funeral and cremation. No questions were asked about the people who were there, about where it was held; who were those funny people with long beards and turbans around me chanting as I lit the pyre? What was in that box that I brought home to his mother? What were the last days of his brother like?

I decided to no longer let the video be an issue between me and anyone else. And vowed to never again send out another copy to another person. The video is still on my desk, but will be retired to a footlocker, a "time capsule" of sorts, along with other memorabilia of Kane such as Marine dress blue uniform.

Barbara went to the 100th day birthday alone. I decided that morning that I would not play act with people. I would not be the grandfather that gets cleaned up and strutted out for a major holiday and photo op several times a year. But I did go up to see them two weeks later alone and had a nice two hour visit.

Our granddaughter, when I started writing this, was 16 months old. We had seen her only four times – the hospital, our separate visits to their home three months later, six months later on Mother's Day, the only time they had visited us since the days immediately following Kane's death, and on her first birthday August 22. They live only a one hour drive away.

As I said in the preface, this book will not end in bitterness and anger. I have been able to surmount those emotions. I found a way through. And I love all of my family very deeply. I have realized anew that I do not know really know what is going on in any other person's life, nor their mind, heart or their soul. And they do not know what is in my heart, mind or soul. However, in those days I was hypersensitive to what others were trying to project – and too often this was not good for me. I felt like a cornered rat.

My Spouse

Anyone who loses a child should be aware that the most difficult relationship with another person may very well be with the one you are closest to – your wife or husband, the other parent of your child. A high percentage of divorces take place soon after the death.

Barbara and I had been married for 35 years and friends for 45, ever since we were both 15 years old. The loss of Kane came very close to ending the majority of almost an entire lifetime together.

My quest was to find some meaning and purpose to life in order to understand Kane's death and find reasons for continuing to live.

Barbara did not believe reasons could ever be found. To her his death was senseless, cruel, and an irreplaceable loss. To this day there is an immense hole in her heart. She misses him terribly. She didn't want to hear about "mind stuff".

Before Kane left for Liberia, he was enthusiastic as was I. This was to be a new beginning for him and we were both optimistic. Barbara felt differently. She told me privately that I was sending him into the heart of darkness and she was afraid he would die there and she would never see him again. That is exactly what happened and after his death she blamed me. I felt this always from the moment we learned about his death, without her having to say it. But on one occasion she told me point blank that I had killed our son. That was the time I went out and tried my very best to poison myself.

For two years I was blamed for every difficulty or misfortune that had occurred in our long time together. I was the cause for the rupture with our son. I was the cause of our financial difficulties. In her eyes all was dismal and bleak and bitter. And I was the reason. Conversely everything her sisters did, and our son did, anyone else did was correct and perfect. I was completely deficient in her eyes. Everything I done previously was mistake and everything I was doing in the present was irrational and misguided. We had terrible, ugly arguments.

Fortunately now, at the three year point, the bitterness and hatred have subsided, but it is not entirely gone. Possibly it never will be. But we are still together and I really believe the love is still there.

The Outside World Projecting In

Electric bills, gas bills, medical bills, food bills, car repair bills, house repair bills. Late bills, bill collectors, bank account statements, overdrafts, juggling money of which there is not enough. Credit cards and bills and exhausting available credit. Federal tax, state tax, late taxes because I had no will to tackle them. Threats from tax authorities. Horse food, horse hay, dog food, cat food. Horse vet, dog and cat vets. More bills.

Piles of paper and unopened envelopes scattered around my home office. And the piles getting bigger.

A disarray of Kane's belongings in different rooms in the house, basement and a travel trailer on the property. A long time before Barbara and I could sort out his clothes, personal possessions, papers and Marine uniforms and equipment. Some went to charities, others to the landfill, just a few special things were saved. For whom we didn't know but we couldn't part with them.

The world projected in on me, was in control, and what I saw there in that world was not anything I found value in. I saw no purpose or meaning in the all consuming drama of that world.

Suicide

Only the truth can be of any help to those of you who are suffering a terrible loss. Suicide is universally condemned in our civil societies and religious communities, considered even more repugnant and incomprehensible than murder, it seems. We do not understand our lives, or the meaning behind creation. We experience suffering much more than happiness. But to self-inflict death is seen as an unforgivable, unjustifiable act. Suicides are thought of as mentally ill, selfish, uncaring, and blasphemous. Many Christian sects and Muslims believe that all suicides go automatically to hell. So those of us who, in times of extreme distress, seriously contemplating ending our own lives, keep this our personal deep dark secret. So I am surrendering this dark secret of mine – for the 18 months following Kane's death, I thought constantly night and day of killing myself. Getting out of this horrible world. Ending the suffering.

Here are the possibilities I considered.

A bullet through the brain. Most efficient, quick and certain of all methods. But awfully messy and ugly for whoever finds you. I didn't want to inflict that discovery on my wife. Also, being somewhat cheap, I saw no point in spending a lot of money on a good pistol that would be used for just one bullet.

Pills. The best would be a barbiturate such as Nembutal. Just as an experiment walk into your doctor's office and ask for a prescription. Good luck. Some people go to Mexico where the laws are lax and you can buy such drugs in a pharmacy. So, this is supposed to be a deep, dark secret right? So to cover, I tell my wife I want to go one of those beautiful beach resorts just to relax? She wouldn't have bought it!

Next best bet – carbon monoxide poisoning. Quick, unconsciousness in a few seconds and death in less than a minute. Trouble is you can't do it anymore by feeding a hose from your car's exhaust pipe and filling the inside with gas. Pollution controls on cars these days eliminate the amount of carbon monoxide needed to kill you quickly. You could light up a charcoal grill in a room or start up a portable generator inside the house, but you risk also killing your friends and family and pets too. Or just as bad, getting discovered too early and living the rest of your life severely brain damaged. Best method is to buy a canister of pure CO, construct a mask and turn on the valve. The canisters only come in 1,000 pound sizes though. A logistical problem, someone will certainly notice.

Hanging – never liked that method much. The pictures I've seen of corpses with stretched necks and contorted faces turned me off. Also, an upsetting find for your wife or anyone else who discovers you. And, if you aren't quite dead and are "saved", good chance you'll live out your life as a paraplegic with brain damage.

My real favorite – for night after tortured night –was the guillotine. I mentally ran through the whole operation of lying down, pulling the rope and feeling the heavy blade cut right through my neck. In my research I found it particularly interesting that a degree of consciousness was maintained for up to a minute after the head was severed. Observers and some researchers during and following the French Revolution found that they could talk to the disembodied head, ask questions, and receive yes or no responses as it blinked its eyes. I couldn't think of a good source for buying a guillotine however.

Poison. I came up with the perfect one, self concocted not bought. 100% fatality. Relatively rapid. No antidote. I just couldn't keep it down, and I tried.

The final and maybe best suicide method I found – death by dehydration. No liquids, no food. Death in one to two weeks. Not so uncomfortable or messy. You can establish your intentions with lawyers, doctors, family members well in advance so that hopefully there will be no intervention by authorities on the basis of mental incompetency.

What really put an end to my thoughts of suicide was my understanding of karma. I would arrest this life without having fulfilled my own personal journey, my destiny. I would return into another human life and go through infancy, childhood, adulthood to then face some similar situation like the one I am in, but hadn't mastered the first time around. In other words, there would be no escape. Only a deferral of the life lesson. And then, the bad karma I would spew out by such an act as suicide would affect all of those who I most cared for – wife, son, mother, friends. I would hurt them and make their lives more unhappy. That karma would stick to me in the following life and maybe more – I would eventually have to atone. No free lunch when it comes to suicide.

Admittedly, suicidal despair does flair up now and again, infrequently but I know that evil little demon is lurking there somewhere and try to remain on my guard. While mental pain and suffering is horrible, there are lessons and challenges there that must be overcome – if not now then invariably later in the long multi-life journey of the human experience.

Death

And so I thought - life is not good.

Welcome death. Think about death. It is your friend, not something to fear or avoid. If you are not aware of death and its uncertainty or its certainty then what do you do? Live, drink, be merry? Bury your head in the sand? What happens afterwards will happen. That's ok. We have millions and millions of species to reincarnate into. And millions and millions of times for each species if we want to. When it comes it comes, as so many think, and I guess that's what I used to think also.

Now, I do not want to continue on an endless cycle of transmigration. But, I don't blame those who do.

Just realize, you and I will die. And so will everyone else we know. Not to be prepared is senseless.

New Understandings and a Glimmer of Light

Balls and Birds

I now detested music of any kind, classical, rock, blues any of it. All of which I had enjoyed my entire life up until then. I could not even try to read a book, fiction or nonfiction without feeling frustrated and angry with their triviality. I had been a big reader since I was about five years old. I did get to the point where I read half a dozen books cover-to-cover on religion, philosophy or theoretical physics, gleaning a few points that were meaningful, but even these were a disappointment. I could not watch television at all, whether news or a movie or a documentary or something light.

For the first seven months after Kane's death, the only satisfaction or meaning I derived from life was in throwing balls to my dogs. Eighteen pound Rambo was my best friend and our 75 pound female Doberman had assumed the role of his mother. He had tennis balls and she had a big tough rubber ball the size of a grapefruit. I would throw his ball and then hers in rapid succession and they would chase after them and then side by side go on furious runs around the yard, circling me as the center. I did this from early morning when I first went outside, until sunset when we all came back in the house. If ball throwing was reduced or eliminated by rain or snow all three of us felt morose. This was my grounding. This was my only real reason for being for some time. The dogs counted on me.

That first winter I decided to put out several bird feeders on our deck. This attracted blue jays, cardinals, chickadees, nut hatchers, three types of woodpeckers, sparrows, red winged blackbirds, finches, grackles, doves and other species. I would sit inside at our dining room table and watch them whenever I was inside. If the feeders ran empty, I would feel bad and refill them.

Throwing balls and feeding the birds allowed me to keep one foot in this world. The rest of me was in another.

My Fundamental Kernel of Truth

How could I, how can I ever, think of my son's death as a blessing and a gift from God? The pain and suffering he faced, the unhappiness and despair my wife and I underwent and still struggle with – these are horrors, not feelings and events that could in anyway be good or valuable. I would not wish them on my worst enemy. I have had to think, meditate, pray, anguish on how there might be a divine gift or blessing here. Even just "going there" took great effort and time. I am still not comfortable with even thinking in this way, but it is extremely important so I must try to understand.

First truth, Kane is still very much alive. His identity, his memories, his experiences are intact. He, as soul, has accumulated all the new challenges of his most recent lifetime and thus as soul is bigger and stronger. In the world he passed to after bodily death he came to learn, or know again, the mysteries of creation, the secrets of the Creator. He is in a heaven-world, free and at peace. Whether or not he will or maybe already has reincarnated into a body, he is eternal and always growing.

My wife and I will join with him, and with all of our loved ones, again. Not at some distant time at the world's end, but immediately after death. Time, space, matter and energy have no meaning in the place between physical worlds. We are always there, even if we cannot always perceive that invisible realm while in a body.

All of us have a purpose. There is great meaning to our lives while here in this physical universe. We should strive our utmost to make our human lives worthwhile. But we should not fear our deaths or the death of loved ones. We will fulfill our destinies, and have limitless numbers of other accomplishments to achieve beyond this life.

To know this now is for me a tremendous blessing, a wonderful gift from God. I still feel deep sorrow and pain, at times hopelessness and despair. I have far to go to again see beauty and love in this world. It is hard for me to imagine feeling happiness or pleasure again. Maybe I never will, and do not really regret that. I have one personal truth of great value, an understanding of souls that is far more precious.

Reincarnation

My second truth. I had believed in reincarnation since I was 13 years old, when living in Laos at the time of the Vietnam War. I knew how devastating the war was to much of Southeast Asia, and was well aware of the massive scale of the conflict, being in daily contact with large numbers of American military active in the country and seeing the B52 bombers cross the sky daily to drop their loads on the Plain of Jars, and return shortly afterwards back to the huge airbases in Thailand. I saw the thousands of refugees flood into the capital city of Vientiane after their villages were bombed. I compared this destruction with the innate gentleness of the Lao people – kind, never aggressive, welcoming people. I saw an evil here.

I went with my family every Sunday to the Catholic Church, and increasingly found the message of a vindictive, punitive god distressing and the Buddhist ideals of compassion and kindliness apparent in the local people around me to be more compelling. I had never understood the Christian concept that we had one life in which to compile a passing scorecard, and those who made the grade went to an eternal heaven and those who failed went to an eternal hell. Seemed unfair to me that someone could have a life that might be a few minutes long or a hundred years, both short as compared to eternity, and be judged for an endless reward or punishment. And we did not really know what the exam was or what the cutoff score was. If you got a grade of 70 did you pass, but a grade of 69 fail? How many points did you get for helping your mother in the kitchen and how many demerits for not helping? If a baby dies before being baptized to erase original sin, why should he go to hell while a monster like Adolph Hitler can repent minutes before putting a bullet in his head and go to heaven?

I had had my first inkling that something smelled a bit religiously off base at my First Holy Communion, when six year olds are first initiated into the Church. We were living in the Holy Land at the time. Before First Holy communion, we went to our first confession, and had all been coached that we had to make it a good confession, be honest in telling the priest our sins and repenting. I, like probably all of my fellow acolytes, stressed out in the days before to make sure we remembered all of the innumerable sins we must have committed in our six years. So, on that big day, well prepared I thought to purge my soul of all evil, I recounted all the grievous acts – hitting my brother, telling fibs to my mother, not going to sleep when told to and on and on. Well pleased with my performance I exited the confessional, returned to my pew and knelt, ready to say the penance the priest had given me. It was a lengthy penance so I was quite confident my confession had been a worthy one. My fellow little first communicant, due to go up and confess next, whispered "what did you get? I said, probably with a reverent, self-satisfied smile on my face: "six Our Fathers and six Hail Mary's". My friend smirked and said "You weren't supposed to tell. Now you're going to hell". And he exited the pew confidently and entered the confessional. Even at six years old I'm sure I must have mentally said to myself "oh crap, this really sucks."

My First Holy Communion went well enough, but the next Sunday, my second, not so good. The communicants lined the rail on their knees at the altar. I was at the far end. The priest, elderly, with coke bottle glasses went one by one through the line of communicants ending with the person to my right, then returned to the altar to resume Mass, ignoring me. Mortified, alone for several minutes on my knees at the altar rail, I finally had to resign myself to the fact that I had been passed over and with hands folded in prayer and head bowed returned to my family in their pew.

I do believe I heard some snickering from my friends elsewhere in the church.

I dreaded going to Church, but years later I enjoyed visiting the Buddhist temples and sitting down, feeling peaceful and listening to the monks chant in one of the corners. I thought about reincarnation a lot. I became convinced that the newborn who died would come back to live again. And that someone like Adolph Hitler would come back too, but in lower life forms, maybe thousands or millions of them. Whenever I swat a mosquito, which I continue to do despite my sensitivity to animal souls, I like to think "there you go little Adolph – payback." All souls have the prospect of working their way back to God. But there is accountability.

I have learned from the Gnostics and the Sikhs that reincarnation is not really a good thing. Yes, we have many chances. Number of lives and times are not issues. There is no eternal damnation. But being born again, over and over, is a symptom of non-achievement. The goal of reaching God, of ending the cycle of birth, death and re-birth has not been attained.

Life Forms and Their Souls

My third long and firmly held belief has been that animals have souls, a spiritual essence. I also am certain that animals have sentient qualities far beyond what humans generally accept. Different than humans in many ways, but no less deep or real. I know my dogs, cats and horses think, analyze, have memory, have a keen sense of time, feel sad, happy, content, peaceful, agitated, angry, upset, worried, playful, calculating, respectful, understanding, empathetic, intuitive, grateful. They love and have varied emotions. They feel fear. They deeply miss the loss of people and other animals who they loved. They question why.

While I know our household animals most fully, I sense that other species have similar traits. Injured wild animals and birds that I have rescued have understood that I was trying to help them, and been appreciative when I set them free. Fish that I have caught knew fear and distress. I could sense it and it disturbed me. I used to love to fish, but now cannot take pleasure from causing suffering to any living being.

Still, I eat meat and fish, eggs and dairy products. Why the hypocrisy? I still must balance my life with my beliefs. For now, I do not want to take radical departures in my behavior that will upset my wife. She has already lost a major presence in her life – our son. She needs to feel her world still has some stability. It is important for her to know a family heritage and lifestyle remain. That our memories of shared Christmas and Thanksgiving dinners were happy and meaningful. She does not need to feel that I now reject the favorite family meals that we all used to enjoy together. So I will continue to eat, without regret, the meat and fish recipes she cooks, until by chance she too has a sense that it is time to become vegetarian, as most Sikhs are. Our human life is not simple. We are presented with choices and must choose as best as we can. The salient point is to do as little harm as possible. To err on the side of the most good.

And does plant life feel? I can't say, but I will venture that they do perceive and have a consciousness. They sense the water they consume and the dirt they are in. They perceive and draw from the sun. They wilt in drought and freeze in the frost. They know when to bloom and when to go to seed. They feel Spring coming and are stimulated to grow again. Plants know, in some mysterious fashion, that they exist. Still, and I might be wrong, but I do not think plants suffer like animals when they are killed to become our food. So I have no niggling qualms about eating vegetable matter.

And inanimate matter – rocks, minerals, air, water. Do they have consciousness? Why not? They too are underlain with threads of God. God is infinitely curious and so certainly must appreciate what it is to be a rock, to tumble down a mountain stream, to be crushed into gravel, to be skipped on a pond. To stay static on the moon for billions of years and watch Earth turn.

Meaning and Purpose

The fourth tenet of my simple and uninvolved, slowly building, set of truths is that there is meaning and purpose to existence, to creation. I had no god, philosophy, belief system, strong convictions beyond my three elements of a basic core viewpoint. But because I was so strongly convinced of the truth in the first three, this fourth came naturally to me. I am still reluctant to speculate now on what the great meaning and purpose is. All I know now is that these are omnipresent. Otherwise, you and I would not be here. We have consciousness, the vast creation is all interconnected. I am. We are.

I am intelligent and have an inquiring mind. I want to know how, what and why. I realize now that unless I am somehow connected, through my soul, with a higher consciousness I will not be able to "see" much more than what surrounds me in this material world. I am confident I will know more. But I also realize I will not know all. God remains ineffable, unfathomable, limitless.

I am content with that, not knowing all. There is more than enough for me to handle right here and now.

The Practice

I think it odd that most of us spend our 16 hours or so of a waking day working, taking care of personal business, playing, relaxing and almost no time engaging in spiritual or religious pursuits. Think about it, if a serious athlete did not train for hours each day how well would the person do? If a college student did not study many hours a day, how successful would he/she be academically. If someone with a professional career – doctor, lawyer, corporate executive – did not keep up with his/her field and continuously enhance their professional knowledge to remain competitive, how good would they be?

So, are the questions of life, death, God, afterlife, ethical living, consciousness not important enough to hold a central place in daily life? Probably many people think that these are areas that fall into the category of the unknown and thus we as humans have no control or input. Going to a place of worship once a week, if that, will tick the religion box and we can then go on with the really important aspects of daily life.

There are devotees of major and minor world religions who disagree and practice their faith continuously – but these are a distinct almost negligible minority. The great majority of Sikhs, virtually the entire community, make practice of their religion a significant portion of their day. The three hours before sunrise, which they call the Ambrosial Hours, are devoted to prayer and meditation. They pray after the work day is over, and again before going to sleep. And in between, throughout the day, they mentally focus on God while engaging in their ordinary daily activities.

This is discipline, training and practice of faith with the clear cut goal of expanding consciousness through awareness of God within.

I admire and envy the Sikhs for this focus. Two years ago I would not have seen the value in such all-encompassing religious concentration. Today I do, because I believe that understanding, knowing, and feeling the divine within and without is the most important objective of the human experience.

It is unlikely that any of us, myself included, at an early stage of pursuing a spiritual path, can adhere to the discipline of the Sikhs. They have been doing so since childhood and their entire society affirms and supports their practice. But, all of us can do more. We can have our own practice, perhaps starting small and then building the practice up as we see fit. The important thing is that whatever the practice looks like, that it be our individual practice. That we cherish it, look forward to it, count it as the most important part of our day.

Remember, all must build on a personal truth. Some, entirely comfortable in an established religion, may find it possible to increase their participation within that faith – meditating or praying alone or with their community, participating in retreats or other activities, going more often to their place of worship.

Others, particularly those who like me find it difficult to pin down what their faith is, will find a practice more difficult. Those people may have to build their own practice. Create their own meaningful spiritual activities. It is very important to do something, as much as possible, but again only doing what we feel is right for us, is true for us, has the utmost importance for us. So much importance that we want to engage in that practice more than in any of our other daily activities. If the practice is utterly personal, there should be no guilt or worry if it does not conform to the commonly held standards of others, even of an established religion that we in great part may adhere to.

How might such a practice look like and evolve? I can only recount my own experience. As mentioned, Sikhs have morning, afternoon, and nighttime prayer periods. They will wash prior, be barefooted, and cover their heads. They will be in a quiet place and there will be no distractions. I found I could not usually follow these standards. And there was no disrespect or irreverence intended. Sometimes I would get up at three in the morning and listen to morning, afternoon, and evening prayers in one sitting. Other times I might awaken late and only listen to a portion of the morning prayers. In the morning I would always drink tea and smoke cigarettes while listening to the prayers. Most traditional Sikhs would be horrified. I do not feel guilty, because I find the prayers meaningful and deeply personal. Similarly, I will listen to recordings of the Sikh scriptures while cleaning out the stalls in my horse barn, again a very unorthodox and probably for many a great disrespect to the scriptures. That is not my intent and therefore I continue doing what I feel is right for me.

Over time, I can see that my practice may become more regular and traditional. But, for the moment, I am following the Sikh tradition on my own – there are no Sikhs within 50 miles of me – so this is entirely my own practice. Anyone can have their own practice. There are no penalties. Possibly an organized religious community might object to you deviating from the norm. But don't let them influence you away from what you think is true and right. If need be, leave that organized community and carry on your practice by yourself or with like-minded people. There are no penalties for searching for your own God within. There are repercussions if you are not true to yourself.

The Saint-Soldier

The tenth and last Sikh Guru, Guru Gobind Singh Ji, was a noted warrior who led his Sikh fighters to victory against the Moguls. He also contributed significantly to compiling the primary scripture, the Siri Guru Granth Sahib, which he installed as the Living Guru, ending the succession of human Sikh Gurus.

He also created the Khalsa, the community of initiated Sikhs who adhered to the ethical standards of what Guru Gobind Singh Ji termed the Saint-Soldier. There were two concepts here. One, to live a religious life oriented totally to God. And to be a fighter with the mission of standing up for truth, justice, freedom, sovereignty and ethics in worldly life.

While we in the developed world, in the 21st century, no longer are embattled communities whose survival depends on a martial tradition, or religious one, the concept of the Saint-Soldier remains valid. There are many battles still to be fought to protect the weak, promote justice, ensure that all people in the world are not subject to cruelty, impoverishment, or the evils that evil people project upon them. A devotion to God and adherence to the Will of God is what gives strength to such a community of warriors, and which ensures the individual the spiritual progression to achieve his or her destiny.

Sikhs preserve their military tradition. While only one percent of the Indian population, they comprise twenty percent of the Indian military. But most Sikhs are ordinary people – farmers, bankers, merchants, doctors, regular people leading lives very much like our own – not soldiers.

Today, for the most part, Sikhs are more weighted to the saint than the soldier, in the martial sense. But they do promote justice, and help those in need. I have only heard of one Sikh billionaire out of 28 million people. They are modern Soldier-Saints.

In the United States we have the U.S. Marines, warriors of the highest order (but in the modern military context not soldiers, a term reserved for the Army), but a bit light on the saintly side if what my son Kane told me is true of weekend trips to Tijuana, Mexico with his buddies. That said, Marines are highly motivated by ethics, by patriotism, by protecting the weak and defenseless. They too are as close as we can come to a group of Soldier-Saints. Integral to their very being is the ethic "Never leave a Marine behind". Living or dead.

Monastics, Catholic, Orthodox, Buddhist and others strive for saintliness. They may very well achieve levels of spirituality that are difficult to achieve when immersed in worldly concerns. But they are by no means soldiers. They have separated themselves from the world and I believe this is to their detriment. They miss out on 50 percent of the human experience and in a future life, I think, will have to confront these challenges.

I am convinced all of us must strive to achieve this seeming paradox – of being a fighter in this world, while achieving a level of purity that will bring us to the next one. A pretty formidable undertaking, but the closer we can come, the more likely we are to being able to say that we have lived a good life. Our life is a gift and blessing from God. We should not squander it.

I and You

The question I have been facing, minute by minute, day by day for over three years now, is how to fulfill my destiny as an individual, while preserving the basic truth that we all, human and all parts of creation, are interconnected?

This has been a long period of searching for truths, meaning and purpose. Answers have come, but in dribs and drabs. Pulling them together into some sort of cohesive whole has been torturous and frustrating. But I feel I have made some progress. My answers will certainly not match those of anyone else, but maybe there are a few thoughts that will be meaningful enough to some who are also seeking new perspectives. From here on out I am attempting to establish a sequence, but did not arrive at the thoughts in a chronological progression. Again, my thoughts have flitted in, out and around over a long period.

"I" is the one human soul. This is the lowest common denominator of the individual. All efforts to expand the individual consciousness must develop from this principle. All else is external to this basic building block of spirituality. All else belongs to one or more collective consciousnesses, into which we may tap, but is irrelevant to the "I".

For "I", all extraneous input or output relative to "you", "we", "they" distracts the "I" from its individuality. Often, human interactions with the outside world are marred by a perceived dichotomy between the self and another or others. In essence, interaction becomes a projection of the self onto others, or the imposition of others onto self. A conflict of some kind is implied, no matter how innocuous or even positive it might appear on the surface.

For example, even with our loved ones, and with the most benevolent of motives, we are inclined to phrase our advice with "you".

Does "I" really know what another individual is going through or what the solution is? Is it a certainty that a subjective judgment is an affirmation of another's individual experience rather than a negation? I think not. In anger, this becomes more apparent.

Wouldn't it be better for one to speak as an "I", thus affirming the self and eliminating judgment on another?

As an exercise it can be very useful to think before speaking and attempt to put a sentence into "I" format rather than use the accusatory "you". Obviously there are times when "you" is the only appropriate, positive formulation.

"We" is almost as problematic. All beings and things are connected in this creation, however, all is not held in commonality. "We" are together as threads in the greater fabric, but we are not the same. Even the broad principles that we adhere to in common are different when seen through the lens of individuality. In the mundane world of human interactions this can be quite apparent.

I have not been able to eliminate the use of "you". I had wanted to only speak as an individual, an "I", but have found that I cannot be of any service to "you" if I don't try to transmit some of my experience and insights outwards to "you". I have not wanted to judge, preach, or lecture but inevitably, yes, I have had to project outwards.

Comfort Zones

I was filled with anger and bitterness at close family and friends who I felt lacked total compassion for Kane or Barbara and me. I was resentful that Barbara did not feel the same as I about these others, rather was upset with me for being angry at them. She explained to me many times why these people acted as they did. She called it their comfort zones. At the time I called it callousness, self-centeredness, sticking their heads in the sand.

I now see that her explanation was accurate, but while she was forgiving and continues to see comfort zones as natural to the human condition and benign, I have come to a different understanding. I was not wrong in my assessment, but I lacked her compassionate perspective. Her way allowed her not to be concerned about others possibly having been wrong, but to see the good in each individual and to value them for that. My original viewpoint was unkind, viewing them as deficient. I had no understanding or compassion for what underlay their behavior. I have changed my perspective. These are good and ordinary people. No better or worse than me.

My sister-in-law Nancy had lost her young son and had endured other deeply personal tragedies. She has suffered greatly and still suffers. She is a wonderful, good person with tremendous compassion, empathy and love for family and friends. She is immensely courageous. She turned to religion to find some spiritual comfort and her faith was and is her rock. But she remained fragile and her pain continues. She cannot afford to have her faith falter or be shaken. So, despite her deep sadness at the loss of Kane, and genuine compassion for me and Barbara, she did not have the capacity to take on my spiritual torment on top of her own, particularly as mine was a direct challenge to the foundation of the faith she had worked so hard to build and nurture. I was too much for her. It was my grievous error – I expected too much.

My sister-in-law Diane has faced immense personal challenges in her life as well, and confronted them with courage, perseverance and a positive attitude. Diane also worked for many years in a nursing home and had to accept the deaths of her charges. Personal and family health issues are real concerns. Her coping philosophy for most of her life has been live for today, have fun, be merry. Don't be sad, don't make others sad. She is a good, kind person. She has been a devoted wife and mother. Again, I expected too much from her.

My brother-in-law John lives in San Diego, not far from Camp Horno, Kane's home base when not in Iraq. He and his wife Mikki acted as surrogate parents to Kane when he was back in the US, and they all treasured the relationship. One of the last things Kane said to me before leaving for Liberia was that when John drove Kane's car from California to Virginia – solely to help Kane – he had also paid for major repairs to the car following an accident of Kane's. Kane told me that he had always regretted not paying John back – but someday would. Of course this never happened. I have nothing to fault John on following Kane's death. He, like probably everyone, just didn't know what to say to his sister. There could be no words of comfort.

My son Aaron's first flight overseas was when he was six weeks old and he spent all of childhood and teenage years travelling to different countries, many of them underdeveloped, unstable, unhealthy countries. His life was predicated on uncertainty. He was very conscious of the multiple government overthrows and fighting in the countries we lived in. He witnessed heavy battles right outside our home and was evacuated by the French Foreign Legion during one battle. He had malaria twice in the Congo and Chad, and an unknown strain of hepatitis in the Congo. He was educated in French and international schools. He developed a strong fear of disease, distaste for dirt, dislike of tobacco, alcohol and caffeine. He was fortunate to meet and marry a lovely Korean girl, a registered nurse, who shared his views on health and distaste for lifestyle vices, desire for cleanliness, order, regularity, avoiding confrontation or controversy. The two of them could be type cast in a 1960's TV show, where the father, mother, children, and neighborhood were perfect. They are very good and kind people, devoted parents with a lovely child. I did not understand them enough and expected too much. I know Aaron grieves deeply for his brother. He is a very fine man now, but will always remain my perfect little boy.

My wife Barbara will always be my true love and best friend. She has been deeply, maybe mortally wounded.

A friend who lost her son, described his death to me as like an amputation. A part of the self is gone and will not return, but one is always physically, not just mentally or emotionally conscious of the absence. Despite the deep grief a father like myself feels, I do not think that any grief can be so profound as that of a mother.

Comfort zones are a protection mechanism that has roots in the primeval mind, not just in humans but in most if not all the animal kingdom. For us, it is a sophisticated flight or fight response. The basic impetus is fear. Fear of not having, or of losing, the basics necessary for life – food, clothing, shelter. Fear of predation – in our world mostly by other humans. And fear of death – our own and of those close to us. Some elements of comfort zones are consciously developed, others are instinctual.

We feel fear and we avoid or combat the perceived threat. In our so very complicated modern life, there appear to be so many perceived threats. We hunker down in our individual, unique comfort zones. Unfortunately, these protective structures can solidify, rather than allow us to adapt to situations that may not be threatening and which may offer opportunities for personal growth and for doing service to others. Comfort zones are static, restrictive, insular. We cannot conquer our fears if even our fears have become comforts and we fear losing our fears. Fear is a basic component of the human experience. But, fear keeps us locked into the duality of the physical world, and keeps us from moving back into the spiritual realm we came from.

All of us have our comfort zones. We need to be keenly aware of that and look carefully at where our protective mechanisms are valid and should be retained, and which ones are actually holding us back from gaining valuable human experiences for ourselves and preventing us from giving service to others. I am not saying this is an easy task. But it is an important one.

For those of us who have been hurt, or felt hurt, when our comfort zone comes up against someone else's comfort zone, we need to shed the anger; understand, be compassionate, be detached. This is not easy, but if it can be achieved then it is a blessing.

The Invisible Worlds

Heaven, Hell, Nirvana, the Elysian Fields, Hades, the Spirit World, Cosmic Consciousness, Valhalla, the Nether Worlds, Pleroma; many names and concepts for realms beyond the physical.

Divination, oracles, Tarot, I Ching, insights, revelations, visions, prophecy, dreams; so many ways throughout time in which man has sought to reach into the invisible worlds. In ancient times these worlds were taken for granted. Today, in an age of science and fixation on natural laws, physical cause and effect, people who are focused on the invisible worlds and tools used to access them are widely viewed as silly or even mentally unbalanced. Those who are most convinced that the physical world is all there is are apt to call unexplainable happenings as chance or coincidence.

But for many of us, things do happen that we cannot explain by the rules of our physical universe. Most important are the strange occurrences that have significant meaning. When I returned from Monrovia, I was a broken man. I had no god or beliefs. Nothing was worthwhile, important. There was no future. There was no hope. All I wanted to do was talk to my son, to bring him back, to know that he was all right.

During college days, I had been interested in the I Ching, the Chinese Book of Changes, but only revived the interest just the year before Kane died and had become quite fixated on its utility as a divinatory tool for seeking wisdom. Tossing three coins six times one arrives at one of 64 hexagrams each of which have a complex meaning developed over more than 3,000 years of Chinese philosophy. But each of the six lines of a hexagram may be in flux, a changing line which is determined by the yin and yang values, heads or tails of the coins tossed. The changing lines, each of which has a meaning in the original hexagram, then when reversed result in a different hexagram. In essence, this means odds of about 5,600 to one for the particular answer one gets when a question is posed. The most sure and unequivocal answer is when one receives a hexagram with no changing lines.

The day after I had arrived home with Kane's remains, his hat, the video of the funeral, and his dog Rambo, I posed three questions through the I Ching. For each I received hexagrams with no changing lines. The answers were remarkable and so directly connected to the questions that I have no doubt in my mind that I was communicating at that time directly with Kane. The odds of receiving these answers to the questions must be so astronomical as to not be calculable. Here is what I asked and was answered.

Question 1 – Where are you Kane?

Answer – Hexagram 1 – Heaven

Question 2 – How are you Kane?

Answer – Hexagram 40 – Liberation

Question 3 – And what now for you Kane?

Answer – Peace

There was no doubt in my mind then or now that I was communicating with Kane. This was not chance. I felt an immense relief. Kane was ok. He still existed. He was not here with us but he was somewhere. From that point on I felt I had one foot in this world, one in a nonmaterial realm.

In June 2013, the night before the funeral of an in-law at Arlington National Ceremony, I had a vivid, intense dream that I remembered in full detail when I awoke. I walked into a large wedding reception, with hundreds of guests all dressed in black tuxedos or black evening gowns. All the guests were dark skinned, African, except myself and three others. I walked down the stone paved colonnaded hall, but did not recognize anyone. Somehow the guests all knew me and treated me with a good deal of unspoken respect.

At the far end of the hall was an altar, with church pews in front and on the sides. I sat down in the last row. The wedding ceremony was brief; the bride gave a brief sermon; and bride and groom walked down a side aisle, behind my pew, then walked through a doorway at the back of what had transformed into a small chapel, no more the long hall I had walked down. The doorway was filled with an iridescent white moving fog, more like a plasma than a vapor. No forms were visible beyond. The bride and groom just stepped through and disappeared.

A young woman sitting next to me, who had been saying something to me, stopped midsentence and then dashed over my legs and at a run also went through the doorway and disappeared. The many guests who were sitting in the pews all fell into deep sleep. I must have too.

When I awoke the chapel was in ashes, nothing in the interior that could be consumed by fire remained. None of the guests were there except for one young woman, who might have been pretty had her face not been twisted in anguish. In a black dress, but barefoot, she was sweeping the ashes on the floor with her feet, exposing a shiny black marble floor. I asked her, "what are you doing dear?" and she cried, "Looking for God." I said, "Let me help you." She responded, "Who are you?" And I said, "A friend", then took her hand and led her to the back of the chapel where the mysterious doorway remained.

A matronly, grey haired black woman stepped from the shadows near the doorway, and intercepted me. With a kindly smile, she took the girl's hand and said "Thank you, I'll take her from here". The two then stepped through the doorway and disappeared into the mist. I was left alone. I then awoke.

In bed, wide awake in the dark early morning, I had an intense sense that I had to understand this dream or I would die. The meaning then came to me clearly in a rush. I had been in a purgatory type world. The few who had passed through the doorway had gone on to God. The many who turned to ashes had been in the hall as a temporary respite before returning to a new physical existence in the world. My role was to remain in this purgatory and identify and guide souls through the doorway to God. But I myself could not go through that door. I was not ready, but I was also somehow a step more prepared than the others and did not have to return to a physical existence for a time. But I would return.

This dream was as real as if it had been a waking experience. I felt a sense of satisfaction. A purpose awaited me in an invisible world. I was not destined to an eternity in this physical one.

In August 2013, shortly before what would have been Kane's 29th birthday, I had another intense, fully real dream. I remember being in bed awake, pillow propped behind me, staring into the dark waiting to fall asleep. My next sensation, still propped up against the pillow in my same place in bed, was that I was dying. I was immediately in my secret place, beyond space and in total light and total darkness. Then three huge orbs appeared. One red, one blue, one yellow. They had substance, but viscosity much like a drop of oil in water will appear virtually round but not solid, inconstant in shape.

I knew I had a choice to make and chose to go into the yellow orb. I was then on a grassy, rolling field of perfect green that stretched from horizon to horizon. The sky was a clear perfect baby blue. In front of me was a small stream of cool flowing silver. The stream was narrow enough for me to step over if I wanted to. On the other side was Kane. He looked exactly like he always did, but he was physically perfect. Everything from hair, to tan to physique. Not a blemish or imperfection. Nothing like any human being on Earth. His eyes, a perfect blue like the sky, glistened. His smile and eyes radiated a love, compassion, strength and wisdom.

With him was my wife Barbara's thoroughbred horse Occoquan, who had died in great pain from a twisted colon ten years before. She was beautiful, magnificent, at her peak, shiny, strong, and with a clear, wise eye. She knew me. Also there was Wolfgang, our first dog together as a married couple, a German Shepherd/wolf mix who we loved dearly. He had died 20 years before, also in great pain, for two weeks unable to rise up. Now, he too was faultless, in his prime, perfect coat and muscles and beautiful eyes. He too looked at me and knew me.

I wanted more than anything to step over the stream and join them. I hadn't moved but Kane knew that was what I wanted. Not a word was spoken, but he knew and I knew what he was telling me, without a word being spoken or a thought being exchanged. He communicated with me in some indescribable fashion and I understood: "Dad, you cannot cross over now. You must return to give Mom a message. Tell her that we will all be here waiting for her when her time comes."

Again, my sense from the three was one of wisdom, love, and compassion. And divinity.

I woke up. In the same position in bed, with a pillow propped under my back, in the dark.

I had no further communications or significant insights or dreams for the next 16 months, a fact that made me mostly sad, as they had been so important to me. I never doubted their origin or veracity.

On November 20, 2014, 19 months after Kane's death I was in our horse barn cleaning stalls. For several days I had had a nagging feeling that I was missing something. I knew I had made progress in some areas, but I was not strong enough to live a productive life. I still grieved and my life still seemed tremendously worthless to me.

Unexpectedly a knowledge came into my head. Not a self-generated thought, not words, but an insight that was implanted from somewhere else, not generated from within me. A channel of understanding. Put into words it was: "Kane is grieving for you."

Then another insight came – again not words, more like a current or vibration of wisdom. This time it was from Kane in much the same way he had communicated with me on the grassy field. He said:

"Dad, you and Mom have been grieving for me for 19 months. Yes, I was torn away from your lives abruptly. That cannot be changed. I have told you that I am fine. I am alive, I have carried with me all my memories, experiences and feelings. My heart, mind and soul are intact. Nothing has been lost.

"Now I know the mysteries of creation. I know the Creator. As I said before, we will be here waiting for you when your time comes to pass over to this side. But you have also been grieving for me because you believe my life was cut short, that I did not have the full life experiences I should have had – no wife, no children, no grandchildren, no growing old with friends. I want you to know that this is not at all true. My life was complete. I fulfilled my destiny. Mission accomplished."

"I want the same for you and Mom. Complete your lives. Fulfill your own destinies. Let the funeral be over."

The next day, as arranged for several weeks, we interred Kane's remains in the Culpeper National Cemetery. He received military honors from the Marine Corps honor guard. In a separate ceremony, Barbara's father received Air Force honors and his ashes and those of Barbara's mother were interred next to Kane's. Barbara had kept her mother's ashes at home for 14 years and her father's for three. In an exception to policy, the cemetery has reserved the plot adjoining Kane's for myself, for my Army service, and Barbara's ashes will be interred there too. Inscribed on Kane's headstone is the Marine Corps motto Semper Fidelis, Always Faithful.

I have taken Kane's dog there twice. The first time, when we arrived and parked at the flagpole circle closest to his grave site, he became very agitated and began to whine, more like cry actually. He was fine when I put him on a leash and took him out of the car. He headed straight for Kane's gravesite where he had not been before, tail wagging, and pee'd on the nearest tree. All was fine then and he wagged his tail back to the car.

The second time, on the main road in front of the cemetery, as soon as he saw the white grave markers in the far distance, he began the same very upset whining/crying and did not stop until I leashed him and again he lead me to the gravesite. He pee'd on the tree, wagged his tail, calmed down and appeared at ease being near Kane's grave, like he was close again to his best friend. I do not take Rambo to the cemetery anymore, both for his sake and mine.

Synchronicity, Chaos Theory, and Anti-Chaos

Carl Gustav Jung coined the term "synchronicity" for unexplainable phenomena, defined basically as two or more meaningfully but not causally related events coinciding simultaneously or sequentially in a significantly short period of time. Many or even most events and situations can be directly tied to cause and effect relationships. Others appear to have no connection and among these most could be termed chance or coincidence. These do not merit much attention. However, there are rare and special situations in which a particularly significant meaning is evident. Such as the three answers I got to my I Ching questions, when the odds against were so astronomically large.

Jung sought to explain human psychology and the human experience according to the scientific method. He deliberately refrained from bringing in the concept of God. Nevertheless, he was also a mystic and often had to admit that there were amazing situations in which some powerful, non-physical forces were at play.

One of the three components of chaos theory is that the more removed in time one is from two or more causally related events, the more difficult it is to predict the outcome. In other words, cause and effect is always present but over time we cannot trace back to the source or project forward to an outcome very far down the timeline. For example, it would be unfruitful, actually impossible, to pinpoint what events in the past were the critical source points that resulted in my son's death. Each possible explanation in the most recent past could be traced back to previous events throughout his life, back further through mine, and back and back through all time – if there was any way to do so. Chaos theory may appear to argue for chaos and randomness but not so. The principle is that like a cone of light from a flashlight projecting out from a single point illuminates wider and wider areas, individual actions cause effects which produce others until the set of effects with some relationship to the original source is so huge the path backwards cannot be traced.

I also see that there is another phenomenon at work simultaneously, paradoxically. Somehow the almost infinite causes from the past, dispersed and seemingly lost over time, are also focused back to a single point in the present, just as if the light from the flashlight, from the farthest reaches of its projection, reverses direction and returns inwards back to the source. I call this anti-chaos. Again, there must be a cause which precipitates the collection of all the vast circumstances and factors necessary to produce a single outcome.

My son's death was the effect of countless causes going back to the beginning of time. Death was his destiny. His life was complete. All the light from his universe had returned to the source.

God

God is a curious word. In the English-speaking world we have imbued the word with a holiness, a sanctity, much as if this is how the Diety calls him/her/itself. Taking this name "in vain" or in conjunction with profanity or disrespect is considered by many to be sacrilege, a sin. I wonder how many people know that the English word God derives from the Gothic word "Goht" which meant a small wooden idol in their pagan theology!

In the 4th Century AD the Roman Catholic church translated the Latin bible into Gothic, and as part of the effort to convert the pagan Goths to Christianity, they had to find a word for the Diety that would fit. The Latin Deus had no meaning in Gothic. Using the name Gudan, the Gothic god, would have been a little too close to the god Catholics hoped to replace, so "Gaut" had to do. This subsequently became "Gott" in German and "God" in the English bible.

Every language, ancient and modern, monotheistic, polytheistic, non-theistic, has a word for the highest deific entity or universal force or supreme perfection. Theos, Deus, Baal, Zeus, Jupiter, Atman, Guru, Tao, Buddha, and on and on. All have or have had an other-worldly importance to the people who followed these faiths. But, God works just fine, as this book is in English after all.

What is perhaps more important, are the other names and attributes of God. Here are a sampling taken in translation from different religions, Eastern and Western.

The One, Creator, Sustainer, Destroyer, Unborn, Undying, Liberator, Redeemer, Enlightener, Perceptor, Infinite, Eternal, Nameless, Formless, Desireless, Compassionate,

Omnipotent, Omniscient, Free of Enmity, Without Beginning Without End, Merciful, Just, Ineffable, Unfathomable, Pervasive, Permeating, Love, All Good, Supreme Reality, Truth, Transcendent, Master, Lord, Father, Mother, Brother, Sister, Great Spirit.

Of course there are many more names/attributes and no religion shares all of the same names with another. What is most important is that it is central to the human mind to believe in something that is larger, more powerful, more organized than ourselves – whether it be an anthropomorphic God the Father, or a divine intelligence, or a non-sentient, non-interactive universal vibration, or an organized material universe that just happened in a "big bang". Bottom line, we humans do not want to think that we are all there is and that there is no sense to the universe.

The ancient Greeks, the Neo-Platonists, categorized humans into three categories: the Hylectics who were only aware of the physical universe and had only the capacity to deal with carnal needs; then the Psychics who believed that the mind was the highest element in human existence; and the Pneumatics whose focus was solely on the spiritual.

I think – and later I will approach thinking as an aspect of mind, as distinguished from brain and soul – I think and find I am a hylectic, psychic, and pneumatic to varying degrees at different times. This is the human experience. I must experience them all, but in order to escape the human experience – my wish - I must not be overly dominated by any of them.

The Tapestry

Words, no matter how complex, beautiful, or eloquent can never capture the depth of invisible worlds, far less describe creation and more impossibly, God.

That is why so many religions resort to myths and allegories, metaphors and poetry.

Here is my own effort to envision God in relationship to us - and creation.

I see a vast infinite tapestry, one like the finely woven silk tapestries that once hung in rich medieval castles. The ones with hunting scenes, royalty on fine horses, boar under the spear, mountains, streams and damsels and flowers. I imagine God as being the fine silk threads, thousands to the square inch that weave the scene together. God is not the scene, but the threads that create the scene. We are tiny bits of the scene.

I might be one of those square inches, possibly a small patch of grass under the hooves of one of the magnificent chargers. The threads of God, each of different color are conscious in and of themselves. This consciousness results in my consciousness. I am not the thread, the color, the texture; but the finite consciousness that comprises that tiny patch is me, my soul, my very own.

In my arrogance, in my delusion I might think that I am the material of the patch and that the colors and textures and solidity belong to me. But they do not. What I do have is secondary consciousness, a self, a soul, that is born of the consciousness of the threads of God.

But the patch is real, and the patch I am associated with adjoins other patches that are connected to other souls, most of whom like me think they are patches too. All the threads of God in the tapestry are connected – from my patch to the farthest infinity of the tapestry. So God is able to appreciate the full scene, the full beauty of the tapestry as well as the majesty of the most infinitesimal detail.

Now back at the patch, I am able to communicate with my adjoining patches, which can communicate with their adjoining patches. This is sentience, not consciousness. We realize as a collective that our part of the tapestry comprises a field of grass. We communicate further, interrelate, meld and exchange our sentience until finally we become, as a community of patches, aware that we are part of a unique scene in the tapestry. And we like it.

We have our identity, we have self-will and we choose to identify ourselves with the image the tapestry projects, rather than with the far more powerful and unrestricted identity of the threads of consciousness that underlie it.

Moreover, we fail to see that, infinite as the tapestry is, that God transcends it, is infinitely beyond.

And so I have coined my own term for God.

Infinity to the Infinite Power.

Good and Evil

Good and Evil come from God.
Pain and Pleasure Come from God.
These are all gifts and blessings from God.

(paraphrased from the Siri Guru Granth Sahib)

Christians have had a particularly difficult time coming to terms with evil and suffering in the world, as their depiction of God is in direct contradiction to evil.

God is all good.
God is omnipotent.
God is omniscient.

But there are evil and suffering in the world.

Only two of the three statements on God's attributes can coexist at a time. If God is all good and omnipotent He cannot be omniscient, because if he saw the evil and suffering in the world he would stop it. If God is omnipotent and omniscient then he would see the evil and suffering and be totally capable of ending them; so then by choosing not to he must not be all good. If God is all good and omniscient, then he must be powerless to stop the evil and suffering, thus is not omnipotent.

The preeminent Catholic theologian, Saint Thomas Aquinas, made the statement that the presence of evil was the most powerful argument against the existence of God. Then he proceeded with his epic 3,500 page work, the

"Summa Theologica", without answering his own implied question.

Kane's death was pure evil. Betrayed by his friends, deliberately not treated properly by his doctor for personal gain, in great suffering, alone without family and friends. Calling out to his father for help, who was not there for him. The story of Christ on the cross comes to mind: "Father why hast thou forsaken me?" I felt then and still feel that I failed him.

For me, to come to terms with Kane's death and survive emotionally or even physically, much less arrive at a new belief system, I had to come to an understanding of evil in relationship to a god, or some governing universal force.

Judaism, Christianity and Islam answer that evil and suffering arise from the sins of man – with a bit of help from the devil or satan. Ain't God's fault.

Buddhism attributed evil and suffering to cause and effect – karma essentially. A countless number of bad acts of an individual accumulated into the present are the impetus for one's suffering. I was somewhat ok with this part – what goes around comes around, tit for tat, an eye for an eye. Fair enough. But why were certain people and events evil. I couldn't find a real answer in the Buddhist philosophy, except perhaps an unconvincing judgment that if we didn't see evil we wouldn't know good, and if we didn't have suffering then we wouldn't know happiness. Couldn't buy off on that – I know personally that I could distinguish good, happiness, pleasure from evil, suffering and pain without having the other present.

The Gnostic Christians envisaged an imperfect, intermediate god, the demiurge, who was the source of this imperfect creation, a separate entity from the good and pure reality of the True God.

The Zoroastrians believed in separate good and evil gods, one of each who did battle throughout time. At the end of time the good god would prevail.

The Hindus have separate gods imbued with different attributes, some good, some evil, some a mix of both, all emanations of a Primal Soul. They believe that we view our world through a veil of deception – Maya – illusion – so what we think we really experience, really isn't real.

The ancient Greeks and Romans created gods or demigods for just about any human situation, good or bad. All were super-human figures who acted out our human qualities and put them to work on earth – love, war, jealousy, hate, greed, compassion, pride and so on.

CG Jung, the Swiss psychiatrist and mystic grappled with this dilemma for his whole career, only once really admitting that he did not know, and we humans couldn't know, because good and evil were overarching principles that belonged only in the realm of God.

An African shamanistic religion I know had an interesting description – good and evil were opposite sides of the same coin. I remembered this statement told to me years before by a shaman friend. This was a good starting point, but I had no way to pursue this further from where I was in the US.

I then came across the statements quoted above from the Sikh holy scripture, the Siri Guru Granth Sahib. For me having both good and evil come from God made eminent sense. I wanted only one God, not whole pantheons of good and evil ones. I did not want an equivocal, weak God who was powerless to overcome evil. I could not get my head around a good, merciful, compassionate, loving God who would punish his children with pain, suffering, disease, fear, despair, starvation, betrayal, and so many of the other ills of this world just because they were naughty little boys and girls.

I knew I had found my religious home. I felt in my heart that the Sikh depiction of God was an honest, realistic one. No bullshit. No excuses. No blame. A philosophy that is both metaphysical and determinedly matter of fact, pragmatic. This world: it is what it is. Deal with it.

Now I had to try to understand the why in this. Most particularly, how could I even imagine my son's suffering and death to be a gift and blessing from God? I had just de-created the evil Christian God the Father and Jesus. How now could I have faith and trust in a new God from whom both good and evil emanated? This has been a very hard path for me and while I am far from what I would call wisdom on this dilemma, I have arrived at an acceptable understanding within myself.

The most difficult challenge for me in my own spiritual journey has been to come to an acceptable understanding of the nature and origins of evil and suffering. This elemental question left unanswered made it impossible for me to have faith in any religion, major or minor, ancient or contemporary. Some great monotheistic religions placed the blame squarely on the heads of mankind – their disobedience to God's will and sinful nature caused God to punish them with suffering. While the devil or satan were evil and tempted mankind to sin, the deific figure did not commit the sins. Only man succumbed and thus incurred God's wrath.

Ancient religions had evil or at least capricious deities who were the cause of man's sufferings. Some great religions extant today but with ancient roots placed the root of evil, pain and suffering into the concept of karma, accumulated by individuals or collectives over a multitude of lifetimes, that could only be dispelled through equivalent proportions of good deeds.

One great religion, Sikhism, does not dance around this fundamental issue. It says that all good and evil, pain and pleasure, happiness and suffering come from God. I have been happy with this theological, philosophical position. It is matter of fact, unapologetic, unambiguous and, to me, the truth as I experienced it.

What has been most difficult to absorb have been two related concepts in this religion. That all pleasure and pain, all happiness and suffering are gifts and blessings of God.

In Sikhism, a true seeker of God should not be affected by pleasure, pain, happiness or suffering. A non-Sikh friend proposed to me that it might be better to say we should not be overcome, overwhelmed, unduly influenced by them. At first I thought he was right. Now, I think the original wording contains more wisdom. We should cross this world-ocean as in a boat, not swim through the waves.

Good

Why, if both good and evil come from God, and both are blessings, should we as humans pursue a path of good? Because we, as soul fragments of God, want to grow. For us, good is creative activity, evil is destructive activity. Creation increases, destruction decreases. Creation expands, destruction contracts or retracts. Creation breaks the bonds of illusion, destruction weighs us down with more negative karma.

We are not God, we are just specks of God dust. God is beyond creation and destruction. Infinite creation and infinite destruction are attributes of God.

The Sikh Scriptures speak of creation being God's play or drama or sport. We are the actors, the directors, producers, stage craftsmen, audience, and critics.

The Scriptures speak of God having a thousand eyes and a thousand legs. We are the eyes and legs of God. As are all animals, plants and inanimate forms. And all of us, not just the allegorical number one thousand, but trillions today, trillions in the past, trillions in the future, all to the infinite power, see, hear, feel, experience for God. As part of God.

In the immeasurably immense play of God, where questions of matter, energy, space and time have no constraints, what are the primal, archetypal principles that produce the drama, the tragedy, the comedy, the tension, the peace and the terror?

Good and evil. All the dualities of this created world can be placed under one or the other. These are the basics. The fractions cannot be reduced down any further.

So why is good the preeminent motivation for we humans?

It is not and never has been. Just as good and evil come from God, good and evil have come and always will come from humans. All humans, no exception. There has never been an entirely good human on this planet. Or an entirely evil one.

Good or evil are matters of choice. We very much have self will. Most of us do prefer good to evil. This is instinctual, visceral. And not just because there will be societal repercussions or our sins will send us to hell. Most humans believe good has an inherent quality, an attractiveness, a meaning, a worth that evil does not embody. We know this but cannot really explain why we feel this way.

Evil is destruction. Destruction can continue until all of a creation ends, but is never able to destroy beyond the void. Evil is finite. It destroys itself.

Good is creation. Creation can continue for time upon times upon times.

Perhaps our individual journeys as humans must continue, lifetime after lifetime, until all we as individuals do is good. Then we will have passed the grade, with no further bars to meet. And then, perhaps, we will pass on to new states of existence, whether in this creation or another, with new challenges to face, higher consciousnesses to achieve.

Duality

Sikhs believe that it is Man's love of duality, love of the world rather than God, that ensnares us into the cycle of birth, death and rebirth.

God is a unity. This world, the human world, is one we perceive in dualities. Pluralities, opposites.

God/Me

Good/Evil

Love/Hate

Pain/Pleasure

Suffering/Happiness

Subject/Object

Light/Dark

War/Peace

Tranquility/Disturbance

Order/Disorder

Systematic/Chaotic

Up/Down

Left/Right

Backwards/Forwards

You/I

We/They

Mine/Yours

Theirs/Ours

Right/Wrong

Strong/Weak

Past/Future

And on and on.

    Sikh teachings are clear that this world is a reality, our reality now while we inhabit a body or future bodies. However, this world is not the ultimate reality, nor are the countless other physical or invisible worlds God created, though they too are separate realities. We need to deal with our world here and now – both physically and spiritually. It is real. It is our human experience.

The Human Experience

"We are spiritual beings having a human experience, not humans in need of a spiritual existence."

HarSimran Kaur Khalsa 2014

My most profoundly valuable spiritual friend for the past three years has been a young Sikh woman, one third my age, just finishing her undergraduate degree in Canada when I started writing, and now in her second year of naturopathic medical school. I have never met, seen, or spoken to her and we only correspond by email.

I had asked her uncle, Jeety, questions on how to understand the Sikh concept of duality. Though fluent in English, Jeety's teaching in Sikhism had been in Gurmukhi, the Punjabi language of Sikhism. He felt his niece, both because of her devotion to their religion and her command of English would be more helpful to me. I am still in awe that for someone like me who has for a lifetime pursued wisdom through the teachings of mankind's greatest thinkers, without finding what I sought, have been so deeply affected by this person's insights and suggestions.

I have always been taught that we are poor, sinful, insignificant creatures who need to redeem ourselves to save our souls; or just specks of cosmic dust, somehow conscious and ambulatory for a brief time, who will return to dust and be nothing again. I have never agreed with either line of thinking.

What Simran wrote me – that we were spiritual beings having a human experience - affected me deeply. I believe this is the most profound statement I have found in any religious or philosophical writing. When viewed from this perspective our lives take on an entirely different meaning.

The purpose of human life is reversed from what most of us have been taught.

I had described to her a trip I had made with Kane to an amusement park. Like most young male teens he had wanted to go on the biggest, baddest roller coaster there. He chose one that was enclosed in a dome which was lit up inside to simulate outer space. The car we sat in first accelerated from a stop to 60 mph in under two seconds then catapulted around tracks that went upside down, sideways, straight up and straight down. A minute or two into the ride I felt Kane furiously shaking me. He said "Dad, open your eyes, you're missing the ride!" From the start I had clenched my eyes shut and gripped hard to the armrests. I opened my eyes and the sensation was horrible, but the lights were beautiful and the experience unique. I hated it. I haven't been on such a ride since.

When I described this to my friend Simran, I compared it to life. I had had a feeling that somehow I had signed on to this trip – I was not forced, but my challenge now was to open my eyes and see life for what it is. That said, I didn't want to buy another ticket for the next life once this ride was over.

My first memory of consciousness in this life was when I was about two years old. I was in a space with no forms, no matter, no identities. There was only me in limitless space filled with the brightest light and the deepest darkness, paradoxically both there concurrently, inseparable from each other. I have only once read a description somewhat similar to this phenomenon. It was in a book by the Dalai Lama, which I read about two years ago.

I had the sensation of travelling inwards towards a center in space. I passed universes, then galaxies, then into a solar system and to a world. I had a sensation of perception becoming increasingly more dense, then of awakening with an awareness of being in a body. Having five sensory inputs.

Being confused as to where I was. I had awoken in a little toddler bed, in a strange room. I got out of bed and walked through a doorway, into another bigger room. There were two beings there who greeted me. I knew I was supposed to know them and where I was. I didn't but I knew that I had to act as if I did. I was in the living room with my parents – for me what seemed like the first time. Throughout my life, when under great stress, I have mentally at night in bed retreated back out through space, the universe and time to that space of great light and darkness. It is a peaceful place. This is a story I have never told anyone, except to my wife, and to her only one year ago.

Simran affirmed for me what I knew, but had put on the back burner as I dealt with the reality of this world. I am spirit. I am soul. So are we all.

Sin and Karma

The bottom line is that sin and karma are essentially the same. There is accountability. There is cause and effect. The real difference is in who or what carries out the judgment and what constitutes the punishment. In the Abrahamic religions – Judaism, Christianity and Islam – God judges and punishes sins. Punishment may be during one's lifetime or worse case scenario result in an eternity in hell.

The Hindu, Sikh, and Buddhist thought on karma is that it accrues throughout many lifetimes. Bad karma must be "burnt" off by good karma, but there is no deadline. One has the potential for millions of lifetimes. One of the unique facets of the Sikh take on karma however is that God can erase bad karma from an individual soul just by willing it – by a Glance of Grace. There is not necessarily a tit for tat, eye for an eye process. God decides. What is clear is that the individual may merit the Glance of Grace solely by genuine devotion to the Will of God.

I have developed my own thoughts on karma. I see three basic categories.

Individual karma – bad or good brought upon the individual soul by the individual human. Karma within the current lifetime is knowable. Karma's carried over from previous lifetimes are largely unknowable, except when a similar situation presents itself, with similar decisions to choose from. In this situation the person, who might have made a wrong choice in a previous life, has the opportunity to make the right choice and thereby erase the bad karma. There is accountability. There is no free lunch when it comes to getting away with evil actions. But, there are always future opportunities to neutralize the evil with good.

Collective karma – again bad or good, produced by or visited upon a group or community however small or large. This may be one way of understanding the otherwise senseless appearing tragedies such as plane crashes, floods, epidemics and other mass catastrophes. There is no way of knowing why a mass tragedy occurs, nor how the individuals affected may be tracked back to earlier collective events that brought about a collective accountability. However, it makes sense that group wrongs would be implicated in group accountability in some way.

Cosmic karma – events occurring on an even more massive scale, planet changing – wars, genocide, extinction of species, creation or destruction of empires. Here, I believe, is where the destructive power of God comes into play. And in the realm of God, good and evil are not relevant. We have no way of knowing why. Some say they cancel each other. Some say they meld together into a wholeness we cannot yet understand – two sides of the same coin as the African shaman once told me. Other thinkers have speculated that somehow, in the realm of God, good and evil are reconciled – still existing but not in conflict. Myself, I do not know. This is not really important to me now. I am here, and good is preferable to evil in this world.

Body, Mind and Soul

Who am I – this flesh and blood, the thoughts in my head, or something else like soul? I have no doubt soul is eternal, vast, powerful. The body grows, declines, dies, and decays in so short a time and really is only a collection of physical materials – chemicals, minerals, particles of this and that. Without some mysterious, nonmaterial quality – a life force – the body is not alive.

What about mind? Many, particularly once the passion for sciences captured the imagination of whole populations, came to the conclusion that the mind was the "I", and possibly the soul.

I have a word picture for the mind. I imagine it as the empty space within a beaker, like one finds in a chemistry lab. In chemistry you can pour two different liquids in the beaker and get different effects. One liquid might turn the other colored liquid clear. Two colorless liquids might combine into one colored one. Two liquids mixed together may produce a solid precipitate that settles to the bottom. I see the mind in a similar way. The body inputs its experience and the soul injects its consciousness. The two mixed together produce thoughts and ideas and mental perceptions. The soul gives awareness to the mind which in turn operates the body. The mind is not life but it does absorb the human experience and transmits it back to the soul. The soul is beyond life, but empowers the body via the mind.

To me, the mind is the bridge between body and soul. It serves two main functions – as a conduit by which the individual God, the soul, can fully experience and "see" the individual human experience; and as a vessel from which the material human being can receive the divine input of individual soul and the Primal Soul beyond. The interaction, the interplay of the human and divine input, within the mind, somehow produces the ethereal phenomenon we call thought. In the human experience, thought can then produce effects – actions, creativity, change, movement which the body – flesh, blood and brain - implements.

So what is soul? As a young child, I imagined it as a sort of withered black prune, appended to the heart like a tumor. If we repent our sins and did not sin anymore, our soul would eventually turn pure white and fly away as a dove to heaven. In those days, soul had substance, was tangible, was a separate "thing".

I later thought of soul as spirit – an insubstantial but somehow vaporous, "real" entity that mirrored the material self.

Sikhs speak of God as the Primal Soul, and our human souls being fragments of this One Soul. God is pervasive, permeating all of creation, always connected.

For the individual soul, thought means growth, enhanced experience. For God, it is hard to imagine what the effect is. Unless possibly it means just a new microcosmic adjustment to the infinity of the macrocosm.

Sikh Scriptures are explicit on the matter of mind. They say that God cannot be known through the efforts of the mind, only through the heart. Perhaps the heart is that gateway to God – the tenth gate as the Sikhs call it which is the same, I think, as what the Buddhists call the Third Eye.

My son told me after his death that he had carried his heart and mind with him, along with all his life experiences. I think it is possible that each of our individual souls contain the hearts and minds from each of our previous incarnations. The soul grows with each and every one.

Paradoxes

We want certainty? How simplistic and ignorant. Change, variance, multiplicity, inconstancy rule. Chaos theory. Probability, yes.

One of the most beautiful poems I know is one discovered in the Nag Hammadi manuscripts – Gnostic writings found in Egypt in 1945, some dating to the 2nd century. "Thunder, Perfect Mind" is a very odd and distinctive poem, not attributable to any one Gnostic patriarch or philosophical school.

Odd, but in a dream where I was given a personal guardian angel – by an archangel – I later asked in the I Ching who she was. I was given the unequivocal response of the hexagram 51 – Thunder. In ancient Greek, the word for thunder is Bronte. CG Jung would probably term her my "anima", or female inner self. The I Ching result, combined with the dream, Jung would call synchronicity. This was long before I knew of the poem, but when I did it struck a strong chord.

Here is a shortened version of "Thunder, Perfect Mind", with lines that resonate the most for me.

Thunder, Perfect Mind

For I am the first and the last.
I am the honored one and the scorned one.
I am the whore and the holy one.
I am the wife and the virgin.
I am the mother and the daughter.
I am the barren one and many are my sons.
I am she whose wedding is great,
  and I have not taken a husband.
I am the bride and the bridegroom,

and it is my husband who begot me.
I am the mother of my father
and the sister of my husband and he is my offspring.
And he is my offspring in due time, and my power is from him.
I am the silence that is incomprehensible and the idea whose remembrance is frequent.
I am the voice whose sound is manifold and the word whose appearance is multiple.
I am the utterance of my name.

For I am knowledge and ignorance.
I am shame and boldness.
I am shameless; I am ashamed.
I am strength and I am fear.
I am war and peace.
Give heed to me.

I am the one who is disgraced and the great one.
Give heed to my poverty and my wealth.
But I am compassionate and I am cruel.

In my weakness, do not forsake me,
and do not be afraid of my power.
I am senseless and I am wise.

I am the one whom you have scattered,
and you have gathered me together.
I am the one before whom you have been ashamed,
and you have been shameless to me.
I am she who does not keep festival,
and I am she whose festivals are many.

I am godless, and I am the one whose God is great.

Countless worlds – Visible and Invisible

We scoff and are amazed now at what human beings have thought in the course of recorded history. The male sun god is supreme and the moon his female mate. The planets are other deities. The world is flat. The sun revolves around the Earth. The Earth is the center of the universe. There is only life on Earth. This world was only created some 6,000 years ago, with all the life forms as they are now. There are physical realms of heaven and hell, to one of which we will go in our resurrected body. Angels live in heaven and the devil and demons in hell, but they do visit earth from time to time.

But how far have we really come? We are still skeptical that there are other inhabited planets, or solar systems or galaxies. We consider speculations that there may be other physical universes to be fun fantasy. The thought that there may be other dimensions – of matter, energy, space or time – to be weird, but good cinema. Not many people really believe in telepathy, telekinesis and other extraordinary phenomenon. Parapsychology, like ghost hunting, is the stuff of TV reality shows.

God still sits on his golden throne somewhere up in the clouds.

I believe there are countless worlds, visible and invisible. But this is only useful to me as a personal tribute and acknowledgment of what is possible with an immanent and transcendent God. I know my son is elsewhere, somewhere and doubt that I will know where until I die. But I know I will know soon enough and that is enough. I can keep these thoughts in my back pocket, but at the end of the day this is my world to deal with. I have a human life to complete.

Faith, Belief, Conviction and Knowledge

"Faith means having faith in someone else's faith."
-William James
American Philosopher and Psychologist
1842-1910

There is a great deal of truth to this quote. Our parents, family and closest community imprint us virtually from birth with their religious/philosophical belief systems, whether intensely religious, committed nonbelievers, or somewhere in between. Most organized religions were set up to tell us what to believe, keep us on the track, and to discourage original thinking, often with the threat of damnation in some form if we deviate.

Sikhs, Gnostics, Buddhists and Hindu's believe that humans can achieve an experiential knowledge, illumination, enlightenment during this lifetime. But all say that one must follow a path, and not an easy one, to achieve this highest level of human consciousness. So a path is necessary, and therefore there must be some sort of faith in the path, and the desired outcome, if there is to be anything more substantive than mechanical ritual.

It is worth repeating: some level of faith, strong conviction, or deep belief in at least some of the elements of a path is essential. There is no way around it. What I do contend, however, is that each of us needs to form our own faith – your faith, or the church's faith, or the community's faith is not going to help me unless I wholeheartedly believe in at least some core elements of it. I think it is impossible for anyone to believe in 100% of an institutionalized path. Each of us will see some things differently.

So I think it key for each of us to acknowledge what matters of faith are totally ours. We should cherish and protect them deep in our hearts, and reject any areas of faith we disagree with no matter how important they might be to an organized religion or community. We need to build our own faith.

I decided I had to either find a faith or die. For me there was no point to living if there was no meaning or purpose or constructive way forward. But all spiritual strength and belief had been sucked out of me when my son died. I had not found any definitive, holistic answers in all my re-readings of world religions, philosophies and psychologies. So I started at the beginning, within my deepest inner self. I asked myself what I could believe in. What I was certain of. I came up with only four tenets: one, I knew my son had communicated with me after his bodily death. I knew this. I will never lose that conviction, that inner certainty. This is my core truth.

Because of that one element of faith, I knew that reincarnation took place. From this last I also knew that animals possessed a spiritual nature as valid as humans. Based on these three elements, I eventually came to believe there must be one overarching and underlying principle, a comprehensive, superior factor that organized creation into a meaningful whole. That's it. All I could believe in – four principles.

I mentally reviewed what world religions or secular world views possessed these four tenets and came up with only one: Sikhism. Mainstream Christianity, Eastern or Western, did not believe in reincarnation, or the spirituality of animals, and complicated its depiction of God with the Trinity, essentially three gods in one. Gnostic Christianity believed in reincarnation and the spiritual nature of animals, but preserved the Trinity and further complicated the mix with other deific beings. Islam believed in only one God, but not in reincarnation or an animal soul. Judaism was much the same as Islam on these points. Buddhists do not believe in a God. Hinduism believed in a pantheon of gods. Secularism believed the physical universe was all there was and that all could be eventually explained by science.

Months before, I had checked out a book on Sikhism from our county library. I had been curious about Sikhism following the cremation of my son, which was conducted by Sikh friends who impressed me with their devotion to their religion and their kindness to me and my son. I knew virtually nothing about the religion, having assumed that it was either a Hindu sect with Muslim influences or vice versa. The book was a short, simple text probably intended for an introductory college course in comparative religion and the only one in the library. But it had given me a good overview of the religion and there was nothing within that I opposed. I checked it out again and reread it in one sitting. I had an immediate feeling of affinity for the religion. I did not have the same feeling for any other religion and for some I actually had an active dislike.

I had been religion shopping for a lifetime. I thought to myself, in old Army vernacular: "Mike, it's time to either shit or get off the pot." Here, time, my remaining lifetime as I enter late middle age, was important. I had my four elements of my faith. Based on these four basic tenets, I chose Sikhism as my path. A religious path is quite a different thing than a faith.

A word picture of faith and its relationship to God was a helpful way for me to orientate myself. I visualized a pyramid, built of levels of stone blocks from a broad base rising upwards to a pinnacle at the top. I saw most traditional religious systems with the complex organizational doctrine as the foundation and each successive layer above reducing the theology to its more simple and archetypal principles – with God being the highest level – the final capstone that completes the larger pyramid. I also saw it possible, under organized religion, to visualize as God being the broad foundation of the pyramid and each succeeding layer representing the theology, dogma, liturgy and principles of the belief system. In the first analogy, with God at the top, I perceived that if any of the underlying layers were knocked away, removed because of disbelief, then all the layers above that rested on the discredited beliefs would be unsound – including the ultimate pinnacle. God would topple. With the second example of God being the foundation, and the beliefs, organizational structures and other qualities being built upwards from there a somewhat different dynamic would occur if a layer above disappeared. All of the layers above the unsound layer would topple, leaving God as the foundation, however, the structure of the pyramid would no longer be intact. It would be some sort of ziggurat, an incomplete pyramid.

I came to feel that my faith needed to be one tiny pyramid in the very center of another pyramid, inside another and then another – much like the Russian wooden dolls that fit one inside another, from small to large. As long as I had the one small pyramid in the center, and was in no hurry to contain it within another until I was equally certain of its validity, then I had the solidity and strength of my belief system. God was not part of the pyramid. Neither center, nor foundation, nor pinnacle. When I finally had a perspective on God, the divinity, the ultimate reality was pervasive throughout the pyramid and beyond. The pyramid was only my own small world and my own reality. Any of the outer shells of pyramids could be peeled away, like the layers of an onion, but in the end if I still had the one last tiny pyramid at the center then I would still be ok.

Destiny, Fate, Pre-Destination, and Free Will

The matter of God having a plan and knowing the outcome, while we humans still have free will has been a thorny dilemma in religion and philosophy. If, in the divine plan, our destiny has already been pre-ordained, how can we be held responsible for our actions? How can we be told we do have free will when our fate has already been decided? How can the decisions we make, directed towards good or evil make a difference in our future, whether in this physical world or as a soul?

To perceive even a glimmer of how this paradoxical situation can have meaning, we must have a realization of infinity – infinite paths, crossroads, decisions, beings, situations, physical and invisible worlds. Once we perceive the unfathomable immensity of infinity, then it should strike us as nonsensical to attempt to fathom all the possible variables that impact on an action, and how that action will impact on other variables. Our choices do matter, we do have a bearing on the outcome. But other unknown factors, which we could well call fate, are also involved in the equation. And the end result, an as yet unrealized potential, is already a reality. Already decided and known.

A crude analogy to this world would be using the most powerful computer assets available to perform a complicated calculation. A vast amount of data is compiled and accessible by the computer. A massive number of formulae are invested to direct the calculation. All is at hand to produce the answer to a question. We have not yet pressed start, but the answer already exists. The answer has been pre-destined by all that has been provided to produce the outcome. Now if the computer is infinitely powerful, and the data and formulae infinitely vast, and the time needed to perform the calculation infinitely long – then the answer still exists.

For us, we cannot know all the variables that enter into our lives – circumstances, people, situations with unseen causal connection to our lives. We also are unaware, for the most part, of the impact deriving from nonphysical, acausal factors surrounding us. But if we can be aware that all is connected in that vast tapestry of creation, then possibly we can be more understanding of how we have an important part in the drama, but are not the only actor, much less the leading one.

Love

Love may be one of the most overused and least understood words in language. What do we mean by it? Affection, devotion, desire to protect and nurture, a feeling of wanting to be close and with, attraction – physical, emotional, mental? All of those may be attributes but do they really capture what most of us hope love means – a feeling of absolute connection with someone or something. A perfect unity.

I understand, feel, and have felt the attributes mentioned but, honestly, love as a separate emotion escapes me. I have no reason to doubt that it exists, I just don't know it from experience.

Love when associated with God also troubles me. The God of Christians, as I was taught, loves his children who believe but hates sinners. He saw creation as good on the seventh day, but seemed not to like it very much thereafter. Nonetheless, many Christians today like to say God is Love. New-Age spiritualists do too. Muslim, Hindu and Buddhist Scriptures do not mention love very much.

Possibly love is the connecting elements between separate beings. The more connections, the more love. Thus, between two people "in love" there may be many connections – physical attraction, intellectual understanding, sharing in "fun", and many other factors. Love between parents and children may reside in the countless connections generated by shared lifetimes.

"Love thine enemy" is plausible when viewed from the perspective of connections, even if many bonds are ones of fear and hatred.

Soldiers speak of love for their comrades in arms. Patriots love their country. Householders love their homes. Some love their work.

According to Sikh scriptures, God loves all of his creation. Saints and sinners, good and evil, beauty and ugliness – all of it. This makes sense to me, even though I do not truly understand it. Somehow, love in the transcendent realm, like goodness, is not the same love we know in the world of duality. Divine love may well be that absolute experiential connection that we seek here on Earth and wistfully yearn for in our spiritual quest for wisdom.

Forgiveness

The ethic of forgive and forget is one of high merit in Christianity. I do not value it very much and this not because I am hard-hearted or bitter. I do not seek vengeance, retribution, punishment. But I do see forgiveness as a weakness, an acceptance of a wrong as being ok. I believe in accountability – a wrong must be set right.

A wrong is bad karma that I believe adheres to the individual soul. Being sorry or repenting does not remove it. It must be neutralized or "burned off" with a good act of a commensurate level. This does not mean that if someone wrongs me he must do something good for me. Not at all. He could do something good completely unrelated to me or the specific wrong act.

By forgiving, what we do is attempt to release the individual from having to do compensatory good. And it doesn't work, the bad karma still sticks. So are we really doing something meritorious by fooling ourselves and the other person into thinking all has been set right?

As for forgetting, that is foolishness. We are here to learn and grow. We do not need to bear enmity or bitterness, reject or shun. We can keep a certain detachment. But by forgetting, aren't we just setting ourselves up for a wrong of a similar sort – either by the same individual or another. It is wise to be on one's guard – not as a paranoid, but as a prudent person.

Compassion

Compassion, like love, is not all encompassing, uniform, blanketing all and everything. Unless you and I are God, which we are not in entirety.

We can seek to understand, to empathize, to sympathize, to help, to relieve, to comfort. To try to see through another's eyes and feel through their heart. Our efforts will still always be incomplete. The closer we are connected to someone, the more we love the other, the more successful we will be at having compassion.

I can have compassion for a mother who loses her child, and through no fault of her own is suffering an immeasurable trauma. I find it difficult, if not impossible, to have compassion for someone who causes harm to another person or living creature and does not feel and exhibit regret or remorse.

I can have compassion for someone who is disabled or ill, who bears up under the affliction with dignity and grace and maintains a compassion for others who are also suffering. I have difficulty having compassion for someone who while suffering is so self-absorbed that they only have thought for their own suffering and no awareness or care for the needs of others.

A more general, person-neutral compassion is much more possible. I can feel compassion for all who suffer physically and mentally; who do not have the basic human needs of food and shelter; who fear; who are ignorant.

Compassion is one of the highest attributes in the human experience, but not so easy to achieve. It takes work, lots of work.

The Path

"The dead came back from Jerusalem, where they found not what they sought."

Septem Sermones ad Mortuos. CG Jung 1916

    I knew a path was essential for me. I needed simplicity, direction, and a confidence that I would reach my goal. I was very skeptical about going along lockstep with any ideology or theology. My personal criterion was that a concept must ring true to me before I would accept it into my own personal faith. I refused to parrot any doctrine or perform any ritual just because it was expected by the religion. I expected that even with Sikhism I would be told what to think and what to believe and how to behave. It caught me off balance that I was in no way directed to do any of these things, rather to find my own meanings and my own God within.

    Sikhism does not proselytize, though Sikhs are happy to offer help in understanding the religion, careful again to stress that it is the personal understanding that is most important. There is no dogma, no liturgy, no clergy, no prescribed days of worship, no sacraments, no monastic orders. The religion explicitly states that all humans are equal regardless of nationality, religion, social standing, race, or gender. This is the only religion I know of that in its expression and practice of human rights far exceeds the American Bill of Rights, and this took place two hundred years before American independence. Sikhism, like the Abrahamic ones, is a revealed religion – wisdom gifted to man by God - and the ten human Sikh Gurus are revered, but not worshipped as deities or deific figures. The Sikh

Scripture, the Sri Guru Granth Sahib, is considered the 11th and Living Guru, and as such is held in the highest esteem and reverence.

To this day I have not found one concept in Sikhism which I could not completely agree with deep down.

That is not to say that I have been strong enough to follow this path as closely as I would want. I know my own weaknesses. However, my Sikh friends have never blamed or chastised me for anything – again stressing that this is my own personal journey and that it is for me to make it worthwhile for myself.

Sikhism believes that God, the Primal Soul, created many different religions around the world to fit the people, the times and the needs of those regions. The religion expressly states that if one wants to belong to a particular religion then that person should be a full devotee to that religion. Just reading the scriptures, mechanically performing rituals, going on pilgrimages will not bring one to know God. The only way to know God is through the heart, not the mind nor the body. And a practice is essential.

The Three Pillars

Sikhs believe that to fulfill the promise and potential of human life we must pursue three important components while on our individual paths. They believe that all three are essential and that all contribute to the others. I find this the most pragmatic and simple depiction of how human life should be lived. This is a universal message, one that can be adopted by anyone of any faith.

First, meditation, religious practice, study to obtain a deep comprehension of God's virtues - a God focus – are necessary to achieve the objective of a higher consciousness that will allow us to journey productively through this life and direct our human experience towards union with the divine. Our inner self comes to know and appreciate the Creator through practice and focus and by adhering to a strict path throughout life.

Second, Sikhs are enjoined to live as responsible householders and honestly earn a living by one's physical and mental effort, while accepting both pains & pleasures as God's gifts and blessings. One is to stay truthful at all times, be free of fear, and bow to no one besides God. Daily life should be controlled by spiritual, moral & social values.

Third, the community is a vital part of Sikhism. One should be part of a community that is pursuing high spiritual, moral and social values and every Sikh should contribute in whatever way possible to the common community pool. A Sikh should also contribute to the betterment of humanity at large and further justice for all.

I do not see how any of these ideals are at variance with the precepts of any rational religion, nationality or culture.

But I do see that the majority of humanity imperfectly, even rarely, moves in these directions. Equally troubling, modern culture and society discourage pursuit of these ideals. Their importance is so transparently logical and obvious, at least to me, but our world today is governed by other, more venial and destructive paths. It does not need to be so. Whether Sikh, Muslim, Christian, Hindu, Buddhist or the many other religious and philosophical traditions, these three pillars will enhance and enrich individual lives and the human collective.

Many people, particularly in the West, will say life is too complicated, too overwhelming with obligations and distractions to follow a simple path to a good life. Not so. We are the ones who make life too complicated. We love the distractions, the dualities of physical life. But at what cost?

The Five Thieves

Sikhism stresses five deterrents to spiritual growth and enhanced consciousness: pride, greed, lust, anger, and worldly attachment. Not so different from the vices and sins noted in other major religions, so there appears to be a common truth here.

The first Sikh Guru, Guru Nanak Ji, said that all five thieves originated from a common fault, which in Gurmukhi is called "haumai". This is often translated as self-centeredness, but even the translators caution that this does not exactly convey the meaning of the world. I choose to elaborate the translation to include the sense of individuation and differentiation, early depth psychology terms. In other words, the more we consider ourselves separate from other people, life forms, and creation at large the more we are prey to the five thieves and fall into the "me" way of looking at everything.

I have been victim to every one of the five thieves, but I feel that after the death of my son, pride, greed, and lust were almost erased. I am cognizant that they could revive and will be attentive to that, but for the most part these were not my major weaknesses.

Anger has been a major issue for me since Kane died. I can expand this area to include resentment, bitterness, dislike, criticism and a whole host of other negative emotions that are closely tied to anger. I think I have made it clear in my descriptions of relations with close family members that I was very angry, but was aware of this and of how corrosive it was to my own spiritual health. I did ask God to help me get over my anger, though I could not myself take steps to quell it or dispel it.

One day, I was returning to the house from the barn and my wife came to door. She said she had just spoken on the phone to our elder son. In the course of the conversation they had talked about his wife and baby daughter. His wife was still having a very hard time emotionally adapting to being a mother, was very stressed and continuously worried. My wife said our son's voice had a catch in it, like he was fighting back tears. This was our highly controlled, unemotional son. At that moment, from somewhere deep inside me, emerged a feeling of deep compassion, and a deep sadness. I did not want our only remaining son, our only daughter-in-law, and our only grandchild to live an unhappy life.

At that moment, my anger dissolved. I felt no anger at my son and daughter-in-law, at my wife's sisters, at my brother and his son, at those false friends who treated Kane so poorly in Monrovia and contributed to his death, at all those who were insensitive about Kane's death, at all the real or imagined people and events in my life that had caused me personal hardship. My anger was gone. I only felt compassion and a deep, inexplicable sadness. I was taken by surprise. I had done nothing to make this happen. This could only have been the Glance of Grace.

The fifth "thief" – attachment to the world – has been a difficult challenge for me to even understand. How can we not be attached to those we love – people and animals. How can we not be attached to the land and property and community that have an importance in our lives?

I have not mastered this area. But a fatalism has taken hold of me that I did not have before. A submissiveness, still reluctant, but an acceptance nonetheless of not having any control or power over all of my destiny. There are unknowns. I have not feared death, but I have and still do fear losing others I love. That said, I do accept that I may very well lose them. Much as I do not want to, I may be the last one standing. All I can do is accept this as my possible destiny, one that I cannot do anything about. I have to chalk it up to belonging to the unknown, unpredictable, unfathomable realm of God. I do not like the prospect, but I do understand that whatever terrible events I might face I absolutely must find in them the gifts and blessings they offer my soul.

Insights
Inspirations
Revelations

Prayer and Meditation

"God does not need to be praised"

Siri Guru Granth Sahib
Sant Singh Khalsa translation

Paradox and contradiction are integral to the mystical traditions – and to quantum physics. Things just aren't always what they appear and several different answers to a question can be equally correct from different perspectives.

The Sikh scriptures say God does not need to be praised. I like this. My experience with other world religions has been that people are always praying, praising, begging, supplicating, prostrating, bowing, genuflecting, groveling and pandering in the hopes that "God" will grant them favors. The prayers inevitably take the form of praise – how good and loving, merciful and compassionate, wise and all knowing, powerful and gentle. On and on. More often than not prayers are not granted. If by chance a requested action does take place, "God" is praised again and thanked for the blessing. If the prayer is not granted, the explanation is that the requestor was too sinful or needed to be tested further. All the more reason to praise "God" more fervently. I always felt this must be a venial, arrogant, prideful, self-absorbed entity to need all this praise.

The Sikhs say God does not need praise. So why then are their Scriptures, prayers and hymns filled with praise and catalogue hundreds of God's divine attributes? A contradiction? Not at all. Prayer is to reach and know the God within. The praise and attributes are for the individual to reach deep into the self and realize the infinity of the divine. Prayer is to tap into the cosmic vibration and expand consciousness, grow and thereby receive the Glance of Grace.

There is no point praying for blessings applied to the material world. Prayer will not bring health, wealth, happiness, security. No one is listening to entreaties from us humans for material things. However, prayers for wisdom, for insight, for guidance, for understanding, for direction are appropriate. After all, we are praying to the God within, who is one with the God outside and intricately connected to the whole fabric of the tapestry of creation. The Sikh Scriptures say God keeps giving and giving and we, the consumers keep taking and taking without understanding where what we take comes from.

Perhaps God's Glance of Grace is always there. We just need the intuition and the spiritual depth to perceive it. And perhaps, in the context of our human, material experience, the gifts of vision we receive do propel us to achieve material success. And perhaps prayers for health, wealth, success and the welfare of our loved ones are not inherently bad, as long as we understand that they may very well not be answered in the positive as we hope. Hope and expectations are a recipe for disappointment or even a crushing blow. I know this.

Many Paths

Sikhism is the only religion that explicitly states that all religions should be tolerated. Since its founding it has been vehemently opposed to discrimination or rejection of others on religious grounds and very much against sectarianism. Sacred hymns of Hindu and Muslim saints are included in the Sikh scripture and these are equally revered with those of the Sikh Gurus.

That said, Sikhism was founded under the principle that it provided the most direct, simple and certain path to illumination and merging with God to end the cycle of birth and death. This did not exclude followers of any other religions from achieving the same goal.

The Sikh Gurus enjoined everyone, Sikhs included, from religious practice that was mechanical and devoid of sincerity and true understanding. The scriptures state that reading holy books, chanting mantras or hymns, visiting holy places, bathing rituals, religious ceremonies are all empty and useless without a pure intention to link with God.

They believed, and still believe, that anyone with pure intentions and focus, regardless of religion, nationality, gender, social status can be blessed with God's Glance of Grace.

This does not mean that religious practices and learning have no place, but they are merely tools for those of us with limited experience and insufficient focus to improve our receptivity to God's communication with us. Most of us do not perceive that this divine dialogue is a constant, always accessible. Our spiritual vision is occluded, our hearing blocked, our minds distracted or dimmed by the illusions of this created reality. Religious practice, if performed for the right reasons and with sincerity, can help clear the channel between us and our Creator.

One of the biggest pitfalls in institutionalized religion and dogma is that it often leads to smugness in piety. Once a person begins to think he or she is holy, they're not.

Governance and Miri-Piri

If we look at a relatively small gene pool such as the 6.5 billion humans on earth, the probability is that they will act in a certain way under certain circumstances. Particularly if governed to do so. Isn't that what governance is – to control populations to act and behave in ways that those who govern want? The larger the control of the governance – empire, superpower, dictatorship, religion –the more closely humans conform to the writ of the governors, the rulers. And so many people think it is just great. They think they are safe or want to be safe; are fed, housed and seek to breed the next generation of governed. Hoping their offspring will move up on the economic ladder or belong to a higher caste.

Art, Music, literature, philosophy, political innovation, independence, alternate lifestyles, deviance from the norm – are seen as dangerous.

But, that is the price of being "safe". Safe from what? Death? Impossible. Happy in a perfect little human world. Impossible. Human history, and, presumably, unrecorded history too, has been replete with death and suffering, war, starvation, disease, discrimination, division, hatred. This will always be the case. Despite all the scientific advances and touted philosophical awareness, the negative attributes of this world are still here. Old wine in new bottles really.

The Sikh concept of Miri-Piri is combining social and political life (Miri) with religious life (Piri). The conviction is that one cannot worship God without also serving people, and that political and social systems, to be legitimate must have as fundamental objectives the furthering of welfare and justice for all people, universally. Sikhs believe both religion and politics must work hand in hand and that one without the other is incomplete, and that Piri must inform Miri, not the other way around. So in essence, Sikhs do see a union of religion and state as being ideal. However, they do realize that with the multitude of religions, and their considerable enmity towards each other, that a state aligned with only one religion to the exclusion of all others is a recipe for discrimination, abuse and despotism. Sikhs hold that humanity is the biggest, most important religion. Guru Hargobind Sahib Ji (6th Guru), who introduced the concept of Miri Piri commanded that the flag of Miri must always be installed to fly higher than that of Piri. In other words, the martial or political discussions must always be informed by spiritual or divine (Piri) truths; that the politician must be humane and just (a likely consequence of doing one's spiritual "homework"). Sikhs believe in taking political responsibility but are not driven to rule those of other religions or cultures. Rather they strive for their own sovereignty as people while encouraging indigenous and communal sovereignty of others as well.

Illusion

"Science without religion is lame; religion without science is blind."

Albert Einstein

As the world's great scientists – physicists, astronomers, chemists and biologists – delved deeper and deeper into the nature of our physical universe, it became clearer and clearer to them that really there is almost nothing there. As we look outwards to the planets, solar system, galaxies we can now see them as bits of dust in a vast empty space – that is expanding outwards. Essentially there is very little there. As physicists looked inwards into the minute particles that comprise matter, they found most of everything was also empty space. And even the sub-atomic particles became enigmatic – solid sometimes, wave sometimes, vibration sometimes, now here, now there. No time. No solidity. No certainty.

The great religions of the East, Buddhism and Hinduism particularly, speak of Maya, Illusion, a veil over our eyes and consciousness that prevents us from knowing true reality. So, if I stare at a candle long enough, or lay on a bed of nails long enough, or fast long enough, or become so adept at yoga that I can stick my head through my legs bending backwards I will wake up and see reality. The apple tree is really a cherry tree. My family is actually big bugs from another planet – or angels or who knows what.

The Sikhs spoke of millions of moons, planets and galaxies; countless inhabited physical worlds and universes being created and destroyed. The Sikh Scriptures pre-date the invention of the telescope or modern science fiction writing. At the time Guru Nanak was reporting on the nature of a universe that we now accept as fact, while in the same general era Columbus was trying to prove the Earth was not flat and Galileo was being tried for heresy for saying the sun did not revolve around the earth.

An interesting factoid. 1.2 million species have been catalogued on earth. Over a period of several years renowned biologists and other scientists, using the most sophisticated computer assets and their combined formulae came up with the estimate that there were 8.9 million species of animal life on the planet. In the 15th century, Guru Nanak communicated that there were 8.4 million species on Earth – all of which were potential recipients of reincarnated beings. Us. As has been popular to say in federal service – close enough for government work.

So is this world we are in an illusion? No, it is real. Our reality. And yes, the dualities of this world are illusory. We think the distinctions and opposites, the polarities are what is important. It is not so much illusion as delusion. We are deluding ourselves thinking and acting as if the truly important matters are those that occupy 99.9% of our short human existence. In actuality it is the .1% that is the most vital, critical and sublime. There is where we should concentrate, on the unknown, the invisible, the Truth.

Justice

Justice does not mean vengeance and punishment. Somehow we Americans have gotten it into our heads that anyone who transgresses norms established by the majority should be fined, incarcerated or even executed. There is a harshness to this view that I cannot help but believe can be traced back to the puritanical religious and social views of the first groups of English settlers.

Among all the most developed countries in the world the United States has the highest rate of incarceration – by a factor of seven times that of our closest competitor, the United Kingdom. As a country which was founded on, and to this day reveres, the principles of democracy and freedom, how can we justify locking away so many people? The majority of whom have committed victimless crimes.

Twenty percent of the two million people in our state prisons and federal penitentiaries are veterans of our armed services. How can we justify this? If 20% of those incarcerated were bankers or doctors or teachers or candlestick makers wouldn't there be an outcry?

I am very patriotic. But I do feel that we as Americans still have work to do. Other countries around the world, which used our democratic principles as the model, have advanced beyond us in some important areas. We need to be more humble and also learn from those who learned from us.

As human beings there is much that we can do on this planet. We need to first of all speak the truth and say that hunger, disease, repression, ignorance, intolerance, and so many other ills are unjust. Then do something about it.

Community

In a theoretically ideal state, we would place ourselves in a perfect community that would allow us to pursue our spiritual goals while satisfying our material needs. But, we are not even close to total control of our environment or destiny – at least I am not. Remember, this physical world we find ourselves in is our reality for now. Not the ultimate reality, but the reality we have been placed in, or placed ourselves in, so we must deal with it.

For Sikhs living in Punjab State in India, following their religious path and the three pillars of their faith is much easier there, in that semi-homogenous region, than our situation in the US or any other complicated culture where secularism and materialism have become dominant. Sikhs in the US or Europe are more challenged preserving their faith in our environment. We, the Westerners who do not have a cohesive, comprehensive faith, are exponentially more challenged in pursuing a spiritual path.

So what should we do about community? This is a terrible world-ocean. Terrifying, pitiless, complicated, overwhelming, unpredictable, unfathomable.

We must multi-task. We must have multiple communities and deal honestly and well within each of them. But, for our sakes, we need to keep all of them as simple as possible. Reduce them to only what is important. Eliminate the fluff. Keep it simple so that you can deal with this world and your spiritual world. If you want to be on the grid make sure it is your grid, as much as possible. Or just get off it and find another grid.

As they are fond of saying in alcohol and drug treatment programs, find new playmates and a new playground.

I do not see an alternative to most of us interacting in multiple communities. We must work, so have that community to move within. We have the community we live in, where our children go to school, where we shop and get our services. We have a community of family. Another community of friends which may not overlap with the others. We are also international, linked into information technology communications. We have local, state, federal, global communities – like it or not. So we must deal with them all. I am not saying that we should embrace them all and strive wholeheartedly to be active in all of them. Actually I am saying that we should eliminate as much interaction as possible while ensuring that our dealings with the multiple community layers are as productive and positive as we can make them.

The most important community, the one that should be our primary direction in terms of time and support, is our spiritual community. But for 99% of us it is not. We try to slip our spiritual life in when we can. We might go to our religious service once a week, if at all. The majority of people in North America, Europe, and Asia do not attend a religious service at all even if, when asked, they will claim to be a member of a particular religion. The more devout Christians, outside monastic settings, may say a daily prayer, or grace before meals. Muslims as a community are more attentive to their religion, many if not most praying five times a day. Hindus place importance on daily religious practice, with frequent prayers at household or neighborhood shrines, regular ritual practices on the many holy days, with meditation and yoga integral to the religious lives of many. Most Sikhs pray and meditate three times a day – morning, evening and before sleeping, plus at a minimum attend a weekly community service.

Make no mistake, for the great majority of my life I did not have a religious life or spiritual practice. I am in no position to judge those who don't just because now I do. I am trying to understand why I didn't before and offer it to you in the hopes you might see why you should too.

The penultimate line is, that despite a great deal of study on religions and philosophy, I found no answers there to life's big questions – the meaning of life, death, creation, after-life, pain and suffering, good luck and bad and on and on. So I buried my head in the sand. There were no particular reasons for me to pull my head out, but I always did hope for answers. My son's death gave me the biggest kick in the gut I could ever have. I pulled my head out of the sand. This was a blessing to me from God, horrible as it was. But this is one blessing that I would not wish on my worst enemy. So I am writing these words as a service to you, hoping that you too will wake up, pull your head out of the sand, address these elemental questions in your own soul and mind, and be less tormented than I was. I wish you peace, wisdom, and serenity for the rest of your lives.

Find your spiritual community. The Sikhs call it the Saadh Sangat – translated in multiple ways as the Company of the Holy, Congregation of Devotees, Seekers of Truth, True Community. At this time I only have two people, both Sikhs who live thousands of miles away from me, who I embrace as members of my Saadh Sangat. I hope for more but for now I am so grateful I have them. I think of them as my soul-family.

Hopes, Wishes, Desires and Expectations

Plus three bucks may buy you a cup of coffee. These are all passive, inactive, weak terms and worthless when it comes to taking charge of your existence. Nothing happens because you hope, wish, desire or expect it.

Only intention combined with action has any chance of producing an outcome. And even with the maximum of effort and direction, the goal may still not be achieved.

Am I being pathologically dismal and pessimistic? Sure, I am not offering sunshine and light to whomsoever follows my formula for happiness. I can't offer such a path, because I honestly do not believe one exists. However, I do believe there is a much better chance of producing a favorable outcome if there are both a strong resolve to achieve that end combined with a tireless effort to produce it.

Detachment

*"God, grant me the Serenity to accept the things I cannot change,
the Courage to change the things I can,
and the Wisdom to know the difference."*

Composed by Reinhold Niebuhr

The Sikh scriptures speak of being unaffected by either happiness or suffering. They also speak of "being dead while alive". Contentment is extolled as a mental and emotional state at the highest level of the human experience. The scriptures also state that there is an inescapable link between service – helping the needy, promoting justice for all, working for the betterment of all living creatures – and spiritual betterment.

So are the Sikhs saying not to feel anything when faced with the suffering of yourself and others? Or to be emotionally neutral at happy events, say a wedding or the birth of a child? Not at all – these are part of the human experience. The key concept is to not be "affected" – overcome, overwhelmed, driven, motivated, controlled, diverted - by whatever a situation presents. All events pass – good or bad, and none of them are taken with you past death. But both pain and pleasure can divert a person from the ultimate goal of spiritual maturity.

Another paradox – "being dead while alive"; and not being affected by pain and suffering or pleasure and happiness. This appears somewhat like the comfort zones that had bothered me so much in others. Or being some sort of zombie, with such a flattening of emotional response that nothing touches the humanity within. At the end of the day, I think the optimum situation is for the soul to dominate, rather than the body or mind. To rise above whatever situation is at hand, positive or negative, and act accordingly.

The ideals are tranquility, serenity, and inner peace.

Truth

"A lie is the lowest form of creation."

L. Ron Hubbard
Founder of Dianetics and Scientology

There are truths and there are lies. There are no in-betweens, no grey areas. But, as my friend told me at my son's cremation, death is the one truth we all share. Another paradox – aren't there universal truths common to us all? Possibly there are ones that will become evident to us after the death of our own body, or after achieving illumination, or after a final melding with the primal soul, with God. But for the moment, while immersed in the human experience we are faced with the dilemma of each of us having our own truths while others have theirs. We do share similar perceptions of truths within the ever widening spiral of our personal communities – from most trusted confidents to closest family and friends on outward to less intimate but still important groupings like neighborhood, town and country. The closer other humans are to us the more likely there is to be commonality in viewpoint, experience, motivation and intention. Nonetheless, no one absolutely shares the exact replica of truth with another, except the certainty of death.

Ideally each of us would search within ourselves – body, mind and soul – for the truth in every circumstance. And then act on that truth. But it is not so easy. We are so influenced by worldly entanglements and the truths of others that all too often we assume behaviors and thinking that is not really of ourselves.

Sometimes we tell ourselves we have no choice but to surrender to the truths of others. Majority rule in other words, or the ability of authority to make life difficult if we do not conform to the norms of a group. Here is where we rationalize and tell ourselves there are grey areas to truth.

The more worldly entanglements we have, the more we let the world project into our lives, the less confidence we have in our own integrity and "gut feelings" of right and wrong, the more likely we are to deviate from our personal truths.

Life is not easy. Crossing this ocean is perilous and frightening. The more detached we are from the world around us the more we can stay focused on the goal – reaching the far shore.

The Conduit

Sikh scriptures refer to a celestial force that permeates this universe and all others, visible and invisible. This force defies description, but Sikhs know it by many names. One is Guru, which is also used in other contexts as a name for God, and also as a name for a messenger of God who was sent to this world to guide human soul fragments back to union with God, the Primal Soul. But in this context Guru means a divine teacher, a means by which the infinitely vast, immanent, transcendent God, has a direct link with any soul fragment. God's Glance of Grace is a descriptive term for a personal interaction with an otherwise impersonal Diety.

The Sikh Scriptures often mention "Naad" as the connecting channel, describing it in different ways, such as the "Unstruck Chord", the "Unbeaten Rhythm" and the "Unsung Melody". "Naad" pervades all, and carries all – most importantly the Word and Will of God.

Interestingly, in recent time the world's most brilliant quantum physicists, the further they went disassembling the structure of matter, became more speculative, and mystical, in their depictions of matter, energy, space and time. Some began to write of there being a cosmic vibration, without form or substance, energy or electrical charge or direction or observance of linear, forward reaching time.

It makes sense to me that this force is the very same as what Christians call the Holy Spirit; what many theist religions refer to as the "light" of God and non-theist religions as a universal vibration.

A few of the most notable theoretical physicists, having reached the limits of their abilities to understand and explain the apparent dissolution of time, mass, and direction when matter, particles and waves are observed at their most basic levels, have speculated that there is some other, unknown force or substance at work, filling empty space. Very much like what early scientists in pre-modern times referred to as the "ether".

Perhaps this force, this unexplainable phenomenon, is the conduit between God and all life, all physical and nonphysical creation. For us, it may be both the reservoir we tap into and the conduit by which our souls link with God, the Primal Soul, in a dynamic relationship that ensures we grow in our human experience, however long and through how many lives required.

A Higher Consciousness

Are two hydrogen atoms and one water atom conscious of the act of joining together to form water? Why not? It makes sense that consciousness pervades everything and anything in creation.

A rock on the moon, in some strange way that we do not understand, must know that it is there. Consciousness pervades.

A seed must be conscious of drawing in water, the warmth of spring that stimulates it to split and send a root downwards and a stem upwards, then to grow leaves, feed itself and progress through its life cycle. It is alive and knows it is alive. It has meaning and purpose.

As humans we may be at the end of our journey in creation. Or at least at the end of this reality, allowing for God to send us on into another existence. As humans, we are at the top of the food chain and have the tools at our disposal to perceive, sense, think, analyze, feel, and understand the complexity, the interconnections, the infinity of this reality.

It also makes sense that there is a collective consciousness – an immense reserve of the wisdom and experience held in common by all living beings. How else do we find ourselves knowing the unknown, certainly in dreams but also in flashes of brilliance in areas where we have no knowledge?

Illumination, Enlightenment, Beatitude, Liberation, Salvation, Resurrection, Transcendence

Zoroaster, Moses, Abraham, Isaiah, Jesus Christ, the Prophet Mohammed, Krishna, Lao Tzu, Confucius, Plato, Buddha - all human beings who over recorded history have been seen as having had an extraordinary link to the divine. Some have even been thought to be divine, others to have been personal messengers of God. I would add Guru Nanak Dev Ji of the Sikhs to this list and others will probably have personal religious figures that they believe were of great significance.

To me, what is clear is that there have been human beings whose wisdom, inner vision, insights into a greater cosmic reality have transformed the course of human history and expanded our awareness that there is much more than what we experience just in ordinary human existence.

Were these just exceptional humans, gifted with superior intellects, wisdom and charisma? Or did they exercise supernatural abilities in a noble calling to influence humanity in profound directions? Past and present followers of the theist religions founded by Zoroaster, the Jewish Prophets, Jesus, or Mohammed have believed they were messengers of God or in the case of Jesus, God Himself. The followers of non-theist religions such as Buddhism and Hinduism believed their great ones to have achieved enlightenment, linking with the ultimate consciousness. The philosophers of ancient Greece and China, Confucius, Lao Tzu and Plato – also founders of non-theist religions, were believed to have tapped into an invisible, superior current of the universe for the purposes of elevating human consciousness.

Guru Nanak of the Sikhs said specifically that he had existed in a divine world and had transcended the cycle of birth and death, but that God asked that he return to deliver God's Word and Will to the people of the world. And Guru Nanak said that he felt immensely blessed to comply. In the course of Guru Nanak's life, he would feel that a message was descending from God. He would recite the hymn or prayer as it came and his friend and trusted scribe, who accompanied him always, would record it in writing.

The founders of the great religions were in a class of illumination or enlightenment far above the ordinary human, I suspect. That said, we ordinary humans are also offered the prospect of enlightenment.

Guru Nanak was the only founder of a major world religion or philosophy to say that God had sent many prophets and messengers, created religions and gods throughout the world to different people and in different ages. Unlike other revealed religions, Sikhism acknowledges that God would not single out just one people to whom to reveal his word. God has no favorite peoples or regions. All humankind is equal.

Gnosticism, Sikhism, Sufism, Buddhism and Hinduism all teach that humans can and must achieve enlightenment during their human life, or die and return to human life in a new birth.

Catholics and other Christians believe we have only one life, but upon death go to a dormant, nether state to await the day of judgement, at which time we are judged and go to either heaven or hell for eternity. In Catholicism, the only persons who remain active after death are the saints. Because their lives had been so pure and aligned with God's will, after death they are blessed, are taught the mysteries of

God, and allowed to remain engaged with the physical world while in a spiritual state. This is beatitude, which sounds very similar to enlightenment except the former occurs only after death, and in eastern religions the latter must be achieved during bodily life.

What about all the exceptional human beings who have been on this planet through history – the inventors, writers, artists, musicians, scientists, mathematicians, philosophers, military and political leaders, healers, business icons, and the myriad members of different fields who have contributed so positively to human development? Are they enlightened, illuminated, messengers of God? I would say no, for the great majority. But, they have received their insights, their motivations through God's Glance of Grace. They have been blessed with a higher consciousness to some degree. In a way, each and every one of us can be, or is, God's messenger. But if we do not understand our gifts, identify their source as both coming from within and without, and use them fully to better our world, we are certainly not enlightened. Rather, we are squandering the blessing of human life.

Purgatory

Most world religions, current or ancient, reflect a concept, a speculation, that there is a spiritual realm that we all go to following death before going on to a final destination. This is a realm where our newly ended worldly life comes under scrutiny and some sort of decision results that sends us on to another state, better or worse.

The Egyptian Book of the Dead describes a complex interaction of the departed soul with spiritual forces, demons, and other entities. The Tibetan Book of the Dead is strikingly similar. The religions of ancient Greece and Rome also held to a belief in a journey of the soul through a nether region – and having to pay for the crossing.

The Abrahamic religions, Judaism, Islam and Christianity believe in a period of judgment during which a soul's acts during life are evaluated and a decision is made on whether the soul goes to heaven or hell. As a Catholic child I was always vividly aware that when I died Saint Peter would be waiting at the pearly gates to heaven. He would have a book in which all my good deeds and sins would be recorded, then decide whether I would be flung down into hell or be allowed to enter through the gates.

Sikhism speaks of God's court in which we are held accountable for our bad deeds/karma. There is no elaboration on whether this is an actual spiritual realm where this takes place - though there are many references to invisible realms, nether worlds, upper worlds. However, it is not the "person" or being or spirit or soul that is subject to judgment but their actions/karma. The soul, the innocent and noble God fragment that is us, is always pure. And, whether through successive reincarnations that bring us step by step closer to unity with God, or through an ultimate divine grace that liberates us from the cycle of death and rebirth despite our misdeeds, it is clear that we must be deserving.

As a result of my dream of purgatory, following my son's death, I have my own personal conceptualization of this intermediate realm. I have a strong conviction that purgatory does exist. While a purely spiritual place, it preserves the sensory attributes of the carnal world. But without the infirmities, fears and negatives of this world. It is a serious and formal realm and everyone knows why they are there. There is true knowledge. The realm is pleasant – in a low key way. There are familiar faces and new ones, but everyone is connected from the past or will be in the future. Here a decision is made whether a soul returns to Earth, remains for some time and purpose in purgatory, or moves on to a higher realm. There is agreement, collegiality, and consensus on the outcome. Accountability, restitution for bad karma, is an important factor in the decision. But, there is also a sense that the incomplete must be completed. The meaningful components of the human experience must be fulfilled before this ride comes to an end.

Heaven, Valhalla, Paradise and the Realm of Truth
The Final Frontier

Mankind has believed in an existence after bodily death for the entirety of human existence. Extensive physical evidence exists in prehistoric graves, cave paintings, ritual objects that belief in a spiritual, "other" realm was integral to the human experience. While many scientists, thinkers, and others of today will argue against man having always had a developed sense of God, my gut feeling is that the sense of the eternal and divine is inextricably linked to the nature of the soul, which in turn is the life force which animates the human body and mind.

There is a perfect existence somewhere and we strive to go there. Perhaps each of us has our very own perfect realm to which we will eventually arrive.

Different religions and societies have had their conceptualizations of this wonderful place or state. While having a strong mental picture of a divine "place" helps humans to persevere in the quest to reach it, dogma and standardized descriptions imposed by orthodox religions only serve to confuse and corrupt the development of deeply personal concepts of its nature.

The Viking picture of a great hall in which fallen warriors drink and carouse for eternity certainly has its appeal – and maybe such a realm did exist for them. The Christian vision of Heaven, as depicted in the paintings and church murals of the medieval and renaissance periods, persists even today. Certainly some like myself, who at church were surrounded by depictions of fat, naked cherubs with wings buzzing around and demure maidens in white playing on harps were not so enthused with such an existence for eternity. The Muslim Paradise in which each man received 99 virgins for eternity always amused me. Either the supply would not last for eternity, or, if they all had to remain virgins it would drive one to drink. But you can't drink in Islam.

Buddhism and Hinduism and Sikhism do not have a comparable place of perfection in which souls reside for eternity. Their ultimate goal is a melding with God and a final dissolution of the individual self. Western religions do not continue to this step, undoubtedly because they maintain an anthropomorphic view of God and the eternal separation of man from the creator.

Sikhism, like the other eastern religions, also describes the final destiny of soul fragments such as ourselves as an absorption into God, the Primal Soul. However, there are hints in the Sikh Scriptures of a penultimate realm – the Realm of Truth – in which all truths become known to us and in which we as soul fragments once again come into contact with other soul fragments who departed this world before us – the ones who in our now complete human experience we loved the most.

I feel in my heart that this is the realm to which I was pulled in my dream, where my son was and to where he said I and Barbara will rejoin him. I feel this is the realm to which Jesus Christ went after the crucifixion and from whence he returned at the resurrection. I feel this is the realm from where God took Guru Nanak Dev Ji and placed him on Earth as his messenger.

I feel this is the realm from which, if God so chooses, we will be pulled for exceptional new adventures, whether on Earth or in different worlds and universes.

Nirvana
Melding with God

The end to the human experience. Where individuality ceases. Pluralities rejoin. Soul fragments, the "I" and the "you" and "us", merge with infinity to the infinite power.

Buddhists describe it as an emptiness, but also as a realm of the brightest light co-existing with the deepest darkness. Hindus depict it as united with the Primal Soul. Sikhs describe it poetically as like a drop of water falling into an ocean; losing its individual nature as a drop, but still existing as part of the vast body of water. The Gnostics called it the Pleroma, or fullness.

This is an unfathomable, however driven we humans are to describe it. Here all is left behind, but not lost, and all is gained.

Here, we have crossed the terrible world-ocean and finally reached the far shore.

Epilogue

On December 30, 2015 my younger brother and only sibling Mark died of liver and kidney failure, the result of advanced alcoholism. He was 58 years old. Our 91 year old mother, in a retirement home close to her house in Alabama, where the two of them had lived together for the previous three years, had become worried that he didn't answer his phone. She had a neighbor check in the house, and Mark was found on the floor. An ambulance was called; he was brought to the hospital intensive care unit. But despite all efforts he died several hours later.

Close friends had taken charge of my mother, bringing her to the hospital to see Mark, stayed with her to hear from the doctor that he would not make it through the night, then brought her to their home to await the hospital's call when the end was near. The friends called me when the hospital told them Mark had stopped breathing and the doctors were trying to resuscitate.

I was in Virginia, awake in bed, in the dark, and reached out to my brother in my mind. His face appeared as white, vaporous, and insubstantial. He was contorted in pain and anguish. I called out to him silently. I said "Mark, it is time to go. Seek God and ask forgiveness for any wrong you have done to anyone or anything". He looked me in the eyes, then his face calmed, no longer struggling, no longer in pain. He then nodded. I then thought out to him: "Mark, Kane will take care of you now".

From Mark's side then appeared another face, much more ethereal, coming as strips of light much like a Doppler effect at the far reaches of the universe. But the face was clearly that of my son Kane. He did not look at me, just at Mark, and Mark turned and their eyes met.

Then the two faces melded, and wisped away into total blackness.

Mool Mantar

One Primal Dynamic
Essential Truth
Immanent, Transcendent Creator
Fearless
Benign
Eternal
Enlighening with Grace

Opening to Japji Sahib,
interpreted by author drawing on
 various translations

www.ingramcontent.com/pod-product-compliance
Lightning Source LLC
Chambersburg PA
CBHW070907080526
44589CB00013B/1206